IT ALL BEGAN WITH
CHERRY SOUP

IT ALL BEGAN WITH
CHERRY SOUP

POETRY AND STORIES BY
LINDA J. ALBERTANO
AND
FRANK LUTZ

FOREWORD BY
SUSAN HAYDEN

QUIET TIME PUBLISHING
Hollywood, California 90028

It All Began with Cherry Soup
Sequel to *On the Life of Linda J. Albertano*

Copyright © 2024 by Linda J. Albertano and Frank Lutz
All Rights Reserved.

Foreword © Copyright 2024 by Susan Hayden

Thank you for buying an official edition of this book and for complying with copyright laws by not reproducing, scanning, or distributing any part of it in any form without permission from the publisher or the author.

LIBRARY OF CONGRESS Cataloging-in Publication Data:
Authors: Linda J. Albertano and Frank Lutz
Title: It All Began with Cherry Soup
Foreword: Susan Hayden
Identifiers: LCCN

ISBN: 978-1-884743-12-2 (Paperback)
ISBN: 978-1-884743-13-9 (E-book)

Library of Congress Control Number: 2024946825
Subjects: Biography, Poetry, Women's Poetry, Short Stories, Music, Performance Artists, Film, Women's Rights, Narrative Poetry, Grieving

Book design by Kat Georges, KG Design International
Technical consultant: Alex Carmona

To learn more about The Linda J. Albertano Fellowship for Women Poets
go to **www.lindajalbertano.com**

Published by
QUIET TIME PUBLISHING
Visit us online at **www.quiettimepublishing.com**

IN LOVING MEMORY OF
LINDA J. ALBERTANO

My wife and the Love of my Life,
a great artist, and
the finest person I have ever known.
—*Frank Lutz*

TABLE OF CONTENTS

Acknowledgments i
Apologia iii

PART I
Critical Acclaim for Linda J. Albertano 2
Foreword by Susan Hayden 6

PART II: BY FRANK ABOUT LINDA
It All Began with Cherry Soup 11
Who Was She 27
My Lovely Wordsmith 31
The Love Ache 38
In Memoriam 42

PART III: POEMS BY LINDA J. ALBERTANO
Reincarnation 45
Party Girl 49
If . . . it's Noir 53
Strike 54
Women Without Men 58
Sabotage 60
The Death of Kong 61
Freud's Slipper Shuffle 63
Ingot 65
I "Like" Your Doppelgänger 67
Progress 68
Of The Earth 72
Majestic Landfill 73
Christopher Columbus Transcontinental Highway 74
Twinkie Defense 75
Look in the Mirror 77
Night Stalking Armadillo 79
No Holds Barred 80
Nero at the Barbeque 82
Friendly Fire 86
Big Ugly War 90

The following seven poems are reprinted from "On The Life of Linda J. Albertano: From Trauma to High Art"
Beloved 94
Busy 95
Good Americans 98

She Liked Her Coffee 101
To the Pacific! 103
Valentine's Day with Lucifer 108
Virtue 113

PART IV: STORIES BY LINDA J. ALBERTANO
The Queen of Teeth.. 118
Flying into Guinea 122
My Safari (Guinea, West Africa)..................................... 127
Walkabout... 130
Nha Trang 133
Vietnam (intro to Mercenary Children) 138
Mercenary Children... 140
The Clash of Fundamentalisms..................................... 142
The Goldminer Manifesto 145

PART V: POEMS BY FRANK LUTZ
Not Forgotten Dad... 148
The King 151
To Dalton Trumbo 154
D-Day in Normandie – June 6, 1944............................. 158
Lancasters Over Canada 159
Perugian Souls.. 163
Renaissance Night.. 164

PART VI: STORIES BY FRANK LUTZ
Carmen in the Kremlin 166
Carmen and the C-Note 171
La Frittata 177
Montreal Revisited 188
My Holiest Day 204
She said "I Want To Be Heard . . . !" 220
Epilogue 233
Postscript 235
An Idea for Those Who Grieve 236
About Frank Lutz 244

PART VII
The Linda J. Albertano Fellowship for Women Poets ... 247
Personal Note 248

ACKNOWLEDGMENTS

I would like to thank the following people whose kind and loving support helped me deal with Linda's illness from the time we first knew about it in April 2022 to her passing in September 2022 and up to the present day, September 6, 2023. As of this date, it has been one year since our second wedding, held at UCLA Hospital, Santa Monica, CA, in Linda's room. The most joyous day of both of our lives. The saddest day came a week later, on September 13, 2022. Linda and I loved each other very much for well over fifty years. I apologize in advance if I omit anyone, I am grateful to you all.

In particular, I would like to thank certain people who loved Linda over many decades, and were devoted to her memory by helping me with various projects about and for her since she died, and continue to do so: Scott Wardlaw and family, and Alex Carmona, who have spent months sorting through Linda's bodies of work in four artistic disciplines—poetry, performance art, music, and film—in preparing those archives for delivery to the Getty Museum in Los Angeles. These folks also collaborated in making a beautiful film showing Linda in photographs and performance over more than fifty years of her life. Alex also has been instrumental in helping me with the book I have created about Linda's life in art. Also, I would like to thank Charles and Tobi Duncan for helping me sort through Linda's personal effects and beautiful clothing, a very touching experience for all of us.

I would also like to thank our ace bookkeeper, Bob Mitchell, who met Linda fifty years ago, and started a musical trio together, with Bob on the piano, and Linda on guitar and vocals. Also, I would like to thank Quentin Ring, Director of the world-famous poetry venue in Venice, Beyond Baroque, who has been instrumental in helping me craft the Linda J. Albertano Scholarship for Poets. I would like to thank Deborah Granger, a good friend of ours for decades, who has been working diligently with me on editing the Linda book and brings several decades of her expertise in the book and creative arts milieu. Her creativity and discipline are invaluable to me and know no bounds! I want to express my sincere gratitude to Kat Georges and Peter Carlaftes for their creative book design, as well as Ashlyn Petro for the final review before publication.

In addition to the above, the following notable friends have been wonderful in their support of Linda's memory: Anna Homler, Nico & Hanne Mohl, Steve & Melissa Crothers, Joseph Staretski, Ole & Ulla Nielsen, Patricia McDonough, Sabrina Gilliard, Daniela Escamilla, Geri Cvitanovich, Rob Levy, Jean Caby, Des Walsh, Leslie Stanford, Bruce & Fran Peters, Greco Garcia, Nick Olaerts, Erin Blackwell, Bill Messmer, S.A. Griffin, Tom Fries, Taj Mahal, Ann Barton, Prince Diabate, Suzanne Lummis, Sheila Pinkel, Laurel Ann Bogen, Josie Roth, Elisha Shapiro, Cheryl & Bob Leathers, Gary & Cydney Man del, Keith & Ginette Koenig, Kennon Raines, Susan Hayden, Suzy Williams, Pegarty Long, Gerry Fialka, Keith Martin, Mauro Monteiro, David Rosenfeld.

I'd like to extend my thanks as well to the following artists for their essential contributions:
- Suzy Williams, singer extraordinaire
- Alexis Rhone Fancher, photographer
- Mark Savage, photographer
- Aline Smith, photographer
- Greg Tucker, Nearly Fatal Women photographer
- Pegarty Long's Philomenian, Venice Poetry Wall at Venice Beach photographer
- Keith Martin, photographer of Linda's last event at Los Angeles Public Library (Central Branch), August 13, 2022

On a final note, I express my gratitude to the friends who endorsed Linda's work and made a significant impact on her life. You will hear more about them in this book.

—Frank Lutz

APOLOGIA

Dear Reader,

To all the talented photographers who captured breathtaking images of Linda for this book about her life, we, the author, editors, publisher, and technicians involved in its creation, sincerely apologize for not having a record of your names.

Prior to her departure, Linda left a pile of photos, newspaper articles, and reviews of her performances and readings on her desk. Unbeknownst to Frank, she indirectly communicated to him her intention to pursue their shared dream of creating a poetry book. Although she is not here, we present this book on her life with a mix of sorrow and happiness.

PART I

CRITICAL ACCLAIM FOR LINDA J. ALBERTANO

SUZANNE LUMMIS
(Founding Member of Nearly Fatal Women, poet, professor, and author)
After we've noted that Linda J. Albertano thrived in Los Angeles as a force of nature and fount of mischievous intelligence and performative creations; after we've remarked upon the ways she seemed always larger than life, as well as—at 6'4"—taller than most; after we've marveled at her triumphant career in the edgiest art despite being silenced, abused, and exploited in Evangelical and Fundamentalist Christian foster homes during much of her youth . . .

We must not omit this. She was funny . . .

LAUREL ANN BOGEN
(Founding Member of Nearly Fatal Women, poet, professor, and author)
Linda Albertano, a force of nature, a woman of integrity, a singular voice of unimpeachable honesty. A goddess who rose from childhood trauma and created art that left audiences breathless. She was my friend. Always.

S.A. GRIFFIN, POET, ACTOR, AND DADAIST SUPREME
A deeply compassionate and transformative performance artist and poet-writer, Linda J. Albertano was without peer. It is impossible not to be touched by the magic of her boundless humanity and love for all.

ANNA HOMLER, POET AND PERFORMANCE ARTIST
She was an awe-inspiring presence, performance poet and film maker. Linda was a great soul, larger than life and utterly brilliant. She was infinitely kind and utterly brilliant. Life will never be the same without her. Dearest Linda, in your own words, "I will worship at your shrine, forever."

QUENTIN RING, DIRECTOR, BEYOND BAROQUE

Whether you knew Linda from her utterly original performance art, or from her kora playing, or from hearing her read, or from simply spending time with her in conversation, she was always truly a poet. She breathed life into language, and expanded our sense of what is possible. She has left her poems as a gift to us all, and for that I am truly thankful. They will continue to transform the imaginations of all of us who encounter them.

TAJ MAHAL
Great Blues Artist

If there ever was a Creative, Very Feminine, Amazon Goddess of the sweetest nature & temperament that this or any other world has ever seen or known, it has to have been my dear musical friend, the late Linda "Albert" Albertano.
Always smiling and happy, so much so
even her laughter sparkled with musical notes!
Moving with the ancient grace of a gazelle, I never once saw her compromise her glorious height with no man, woman,
child or musician!
Absolutely stunning
woman!
She wrote volumes of poetry, songs, was a wonderful performance artist,
played guitar, sang
and so much more!

I was recently able to play one of my all time favorite songs of Linda's, called "2:10 Train"
This concert, which featured The Taj Mahal Quartet and a
very lovely friend from both our pasts named Pamela Poland!
The combination of the quartet, Pamela's strong performance, warm and soothing voice & vocal, mesmerized
the sold out audience!
They responded with thunderous applause!
Thrilled doesn't even come close to how it felt!
We KNOW SHE heard us!!:))
Peace & Beauty
(Rest In Power)

PRINCE DIABATE, KORA MASTER GUINEA, WEST AFRICA.
(Translated from the French by Frank Lutz.)

For my Big Sister Linda J. Albertano, my advisor, my student, she was a Grand Lady, very special in my life. I am composing your song, my sister Linda's song in the Zone of the Spirit and with us. Thank you very much, my Linda, from my heart, and with gratitude. Your kora instructor since 1999.

Prince Diabate, is known in Africa as Kora Master

ADAM LEIPZIG
Producer, director, stage, and performance art productions

When we opened the Los Angeles Theatre Center in 1985, performance art had already matured and was moving forward along different and divergent pathways. We had to do a performance art series and we had to get Linda J. Albertano. Linda was flattered to be asked, surprised even, which surprised me, because I had only seen her in performance, and her work struck me as so singular she'd be difficult to convince. "What do you do there?" Linda asked me. "I'm the dramaturg and producing this series," I said. "Of course I'll do it," said Linda. She even knew what a dramaturg was!

Of performance art's divergent pathways at the time, Linda had made the unequivocal decision for performance. She talked, she sang, she moved. She spoke poetry, changed costumes and characters. She had the capacity concentrate herself and expand herself into each situation. When she concentrated herself, her body reduced, became smaller and more vulnerable. This was part of her art, because in life she was taller than most everyone around. When she expanded, you could have sworn she was eight feet tall.

Did I mention the marching band? Yes, there was a marching band. Thirty high schoolers from South LA, dancers, and poets too, all brought together by Linda for her epic piece "Joan of Compton." The band was out in front on Spring Street, drums beating time as they warmed up. Across the street, windows opened at the Alexandria Hotel, a hotel that had once been grand but was now SRO, windows opened, curses hurled, empty 7 Crown bottles hurled too, glass shattered everywhere. We brought the band inside, and Joan of Compton went on. This performance of identity and sacrifice, interrogating the role of women, of suburbs' contrast with central city, of self-realization and self-abnegation being a white person in diverse society.

Where was the truest performance, Linda wondered later, in our 99-seat black box theatre, or in the glass on asphalt outside?

In more recent years we had the privilege of publishing some of Linda's poems in Cultural Daily, and her memories of performing for USO in Vietnam. Whether in words written or spoken, in poetry or prose, in music and in physical presence, her light transcended shape and form. That was her pathway!

PETER CARLAFTES & KAT GEORGES
Poets, publishers and leaders in the Dada art movement

Linda Albertano was a one-of-a-kind artist and human being. Her poetry and performance art was so earth-shatteringly original, it made us all aspire to raise the stakes of our own work. But an artist is more than their art, and Linda was equally defined by her kindness, her humor, and her indefatigable support of other creators. For many years, Linda has been a beloved member of our worldwide Dada family, performing with us in Los Angeles, San Francisco, and New Orleans, with original work, in a staged reading, embodying New York Dada legend Baroness Elsa von Freytag Loringhoven, and more. We miss her daily, and thrive on the memory of our time together.

FOREWORD

BY SUSAN HAYDEN

There's a statue in Florence, Italy, at the Basilica of Santa Croce, that reminds me of Linda Albertano. It is known as *The Liberty of Poetry*. It has a crown of eight rays and in its left hand, holds a lyre and a laurel wreath, symbolizing the glory of poetry. Its right hand lifts a broken chain. It is believed to be the inspiration for (and predecessor of) our own Statue of Liberty. It was intended to represent "the freedom of art and creative genius in general." And wasn't that Linda, who embodied the essence of such ideals?

The truth is, I was on the periphery of Linda's life. And when I arrived on the spoken word scene in the late 1980s, I felt intimidated by her. It was a stature issue—not her height so much as the magnitude of her presence, the breadth of her work. She was majestic. She was almighty.

My intimidation was short-lived, as she welcomed me the way she greeted all artists: with those lanky open arms, eyes with answers and an unlocked heart. Our worlds seemed to continually overlap. When she would come read at my show, *Library Girl*, her fierce tenderness enlivened and ignited the room. When she invited me to share my poems and be the subject of a *TribeLA* Acrostic Interview, I felt, as Anne Lamott once wrote, "fished out of the rubble."

The way she lived her own creative life, on *her* terms, gives reassurance to be our fullest, most realized selves. The way she valued and joyously responded to that creative impulse in all of us is a template for literary citizenship. She has been, and will remain, a beacon to me.

She was illuminated from the inside out. To behold her felt like standing in the center of the Eiffel Tower at night, during that first five minutes at the top of the hour, when it's golden and sparkling with twenty thousand flashing lights. Being near Linda was like being inside lightning.

(Note: The above-referenced Florentine statue was carved by Pio Fedi and dedicated to poet-playwright of the Risorgimento, Giovanni Battista Niccolini.)

ABOUT SUSAN HAYDEN

Susan Hayden is a multigenre writer. Her debut book, *Now You Are a Missing Person*, a hybrid memoir in poems, stories and fragments, was published in 2023 by Moon Tide Press. It received a Kirkus Star from *Kirkus Reviews* and was included in the Best of 2023: Fiction & Literature from Los Angeles Public Library. It was a finalist in the Eric Hoffer Award 2024, a finalist in the 18th Annual National Indie Excellence Awards and a finalist in The Zibby Awards 2023. Most recently, *Now You Are a Missing Person* made the shortlist for The Memoir Prize for Books.

Hayden's work has been included in the anthologies *From Venice to Venice: Poets of California and Italy* (El Martillo Press, 2024); *Beat Not Beat* (Moon Tide Press); *Los Angeles In the 1970s: Weird Scenes Inside the Goldmine* (Rare Bird Books); *The Black Body* (Seven Stories Press) and elsewhere.

She is the creator and producer of the long-running, monthly literary series, Library Girl at Ruskin Group Theatre. In 2015, she received the Bruria Finkel/Artist in the Community Volunteerism Award from the Santa Monica Arts Foundation, for her "significant contributions to the energetic discourse within Santa Monica's arts community."

The proud mother of singer-songwriter Mason Summit, she lives in Santa Monica with her husband, music journalist Steve Hochman.

PART II
BY FRANK, ABOUT LINDA

Linda's husband, Frank, wrote the introduction
"It All Began with Cherry Soup" and these three poems
in the final year of her life.

IT ALL BEGAN WITH CHERRY SOUP

It was a beautiful Southern California neighborhood, but I had already, at my young age, seen enough beauty around the world to fill a lifetime. I had only arrived in West Hollywood the first week of January. Actually, after all my travels, I was wondering why I had come out to Hollywood, anyway.

But this lousy night in the West Hollywood–Beverly Hills neighborhood where I was staying, that is, renting a room, I was about half a block east of North Doheny Drive and Sunset Boulevard standing on the curbside trying to hitch a ride at rush hour. It was February 1968, in the dead of winter. The evening was dark, cold, wet with rain, and miserable. I was holding my leather jacket over my head, hoping that one of the thousands of passing cars would stop soon to keep me from getting too wet. Fat chance.

It was 6:15 in the evening and I needed to go east into Hollywood and the Cahuenga Hills to my manager Byron's home. His old house, once owned by the famous early movie star and heart throb, Rudolph Valentino, was a few miles away. I needed to be there by 7:00pm on this Monday evening, as that was his weekly meeting time to gather his young talent together to rehearse scenes and learn acting techniques for film work and television. During the week, Byron would send us out on talent calls to local movie and TV studios to get us work.

This introduction, *It All Began with Cherry Soup*, tells the story of how Linda and I met. I start here because this alone was magical and set up our relationship, which lasted for five and one-half decades, until she passed away on 9/13/2022, leaving us all bereft of a great artist and loving human friend. Linda J. Albertano was a fabulous and much honored artist of poetry, performance art, music, and film from Venice, California. She was a wonderful person who was my companion, partner, and wife.

After about five minutes of standing in the rain with my thumb out, I heard some loud honk-honk-honking behind me, but for some reason did not turn around to look. I was sort of assuming it was just traffic noise from the multitude of cars passing. Maybe I was just on the duh-channel. A few seconds later the honk-honk-HONKING repeated itself, this time louder and prolonged. So I turned around quickly to see if it was for me. About fifty feet away I saw a '53 Mercury straight-eight Coupe, red body and gray top, stopped. Sticking out of the passenger window and beckoning me forward was a long arm, I presumed belonging to a passenger. I ran up to the car and looked into the open window. There was no passenger, only a very tall young lady about my age in the driver's seat. She said to me, "C'mon, get in out of the rain!" which I gladly did. Then, "Where you headed?" she said.

"To Cahuenga Boulevard."

I settled into the passenger seat and looked over to my left and was stunned by the length of her body and legs, and the beauty of her face. She was wearing a culotte skirt, a shirt and jacket, and low-cut tennies. At this time in history, it was normal for young people to pick up hitchhikers as all of the kids were thinking the same way: against the war in Vietnam, Civil Rights for everybody in our own country, and listening to Bob Dylan's social commentary music.

"Hi, my name's Frank. What's yours?"

"Linda."

Silence.

"Uh, you wanna stop and get some coffee?"

"No."

Silence.

What did she mean "no"? No? No? Next, what's my next line gonna be? I had by then completely forgotten about Byron's meeting. Whoosh! Now I was thinking about my next line, to get this gorgeous dame to stop and have coffee with me.

Then: "But I'll stop and have tea and cherry soup with you."

"Cherry soup? Cool! Let's do it!"

I knew all about cherry soup. Because for several years before meeting Linda, I had gone back and forth to universities in Europe. In addition to France, there would be Italy and then Germany. During the summers between school, a great Danish friend of mine, Nico, who I had first met in school in France got me a summer job on a farm near his home in Denmark. So I learned some Danish and earned some money for school. In Denmark they grow beautiful red cherries.

They harvest them, blanch them for a minute in boiling water, cool and seed them, mash them, and add some honey, then some hot water and gelatin, and cool the whole mix in the fridge. It comes out as a sort of cherry Jell-o that is served cold with cream on top. Absolutely delicious!

"OK. There's a Greek restaurant on Cahuenga where they serve it. We'll go there."

The Danes love the Greeks because the Greeks immigrate to Denmark and do what? . . . open restaurants and serve their great food to the Danes. But they also learned about cherry soup from the Danes, and voila! A Greek restaurant in Hollywood serving Danish cherry soup! And of course, by this time, Byron no longer existed!

As we parked and got out of her car, I could see how tall she was, about two inches shorter than me! And shaped like a model. We entered and sat at the bar. Beyond us, in a large open room, recorded Greek music was playing and men were drinking Ouzo and Retsina, and dancing their circle folk dance. We ordered tea and cherry soup and started to talk.

I asked her: "So whadya do for a living?"

"Oh, this and that. I work part-time in a restaurant as a waitress, and in another place as a hostess. And teach some music and write songs."

"Nice."

"What about you?"

"I'm sorta new in LA, since early January. I was brought out here as an actor, so I work nights so I can go out on acting job calls during the day. I'm supposed to be going to a meeting this evening at my manager Byron's house, but this is more interesting."

"You've only been out here since early January, and you already have a manager?"

"Yep. Well, he had seen me on stage in a play last August at the repertory summer theatre outside the beautiful amphitheater at Antioch College in Yellow Springs, Ohio. The play, by Jean Genet, the great French playwright was *The Balcony*."

"Yes, I know who Genet is."

"Oh, good. Anyway, after the play he introduced himself, very nice person, and told me he could get me work out here. I wasn't interested at first. I had been doing stage acting in between school in Europe, have done a little in New York City, and I wanted to go back there."

"Why didn't you?"

"Go back to New York?"

"Yes."

"Well, shortly after I met Byron, my dad died. That was awful. So I stayed around at Antioch for the autumn, studied theatre there, and roomed with my dear buddy Bart. But at Christmastime I thought, Why not try LA? Byron said he would help me out with some money to come out here. So I came out after the first of this year."

"So has he got you any work?"

"Not yet. Some calls. And late this week I go back to the *Bonanza* set for a second interview."

"So how are you supporting yourself? Rich parents? I'm sorry, I mean, rich Mom?"

"No way. No, I got a night job out here at Cedars-Sinai Hospital, on the psychiatric ward. Psychiatric Technician."

"Howd-ja get that?"

"I'm a Combat Medic NCO in the US Air Force Reserves. We get trained in battlefield medicine, including psychiatric. We do more than civilian nursing personnel are authorized to do. Cedars-Sinai knew that. And that hospital is not far from where I'm staying."

"Cool. Sounds more interesting than my jobs. Although I'm applying for a job at the UCLA Map Library."

"Are you going to school at UCLA?"

"Yep."

"Wow. That's a great university."

"Sure is."

"What are you studying?"

"I started out at UC Irvine studying nutrition. But I'm not very impressed with the way academics go at nutrition. I'm more interested in art anyway. So I switched to philosophy and film at UCLA. My major is film."

"Very cool! Great place to study it. So have you taken art as well as film classes?"

"No. I'm really interested in learning the auteur system and methods of filmmaking. Lotta work. How about you? Where'd you go to college?"

"Uh, actually I've been to five universities, three in Europe and two in the USA."

"Really? What were you studying in all those places?"

"Well, I started out at Ohio State, got hurt in my second year playing football, so I got the year off, and so, I went to school in France. Paris. But before Paris, and after, I worked for a while in oceanography, sailed around the world. Then I went back to school in Italy, then Germany."

"What were you studying?"

"European languages."

"Did you get a degree?"

"Not yet. I had planned to, but by accident I fell into acting, found out I could make a living at it, and that's what brought me out here."

"How did you fall into acting by accident?"

"Oh, it's a long story. Early in 1965 I was back in my hometown of Dayton, Ohio from studies in Europe—Germany. A buddy of mine, Jon, was in the community theatre, a good actor, and he had an audition for a lead part in a local playhouse. He invited me to come along. So I did. We got to the theatre, and were assembled with all the actors, waiting for auditions to begin. But another guy who was supposed to play an opposing lead to my friend didn't show up. So the director, an easy going guy, asked me if I would like to just read the other guy's part. I said, sure, why not? So I did, never having seen the script before. The director set up the scene and told us what pages to read. When I read my part, the director stopped us for a minute, asked me if I had ever been in a play before, I said no. He asked me to go on reading a couple of pages, of my part, with him, the director, reading my friend's part. After a few minutes, he stopped me, and complimented me, and said that I was a natural "sight reader." He told me that meant that I could see a script and get it immediately. He said I did a good job, and invited me to play that part, if I would like to do so. Being fearless, I said yes, I would be happy to play the part."

"Cool! What was the play?"

"It was *Look Back in Anger* by John Osborne. I played Jimmy. It was made into a film in the late '50s starring Richard Burton."

"Yes, and Jimmy was the lead character."

"Which was the part my buddy was supposed to play. But he got the winter flu!"

"So, lucky you."

"Yep. In any event, that spring, '65, my buddy told me that Antioch College in Yellow Springs, Ohio was holding auditions for Summer Stock theatre, for the whole repertory group to do five plays in ten weeks. He was going to audition and suggested that I do the same. So we went out to Antioch together, and they hired both of us. The first year I was an apprentice actor. We would work on sets constructing them for the stage, and rehearse plays in the evening, until the season started. Once we were doing a play each night for two weeks, we would rehearse the upcoming play during the days. It was great."

"I should think. So did you do the next summer at Antioch, too?"

"Yes, '66 and '67, which is when Byron saw me on stage. By then I was getting the good parts to play. But enough about me. Tell me about you. So you're at UCLA, plus you're working two part time jobs, plus . . . "

"Plus, I'm teaching guitar in my spare time."

"Jesus! I'm impressed! But you're so gorgeous, you should be a model. You remind me of Varushka, who was 6'3" and gorgeous, too. How tall are you?"

"I'm about 6'4."

"Wow. I'm right at 6'6"

"I have modelled before, but it's not steady work. And very eccentric, with egos, and so forth. But yes, I do some modeling, too."

"Great. And yes, I've heard the modelling industry can be rough."

"By the way, shouldn't we be getting you to Byron's? It's already after 7:00pm."

"Oh, hell, just when we're having fun. Why don't you come with me? I'll introduce you."

"Maybe another time. I need to get home and study."

"OK. Do you have a phone?"

"No."

"Neither do I. At least you have a car, I have yet to get one. Do you have school tomorrow?"

"No."

"Wanna go have lunch with me tomorrow?"

"OK. Around noon?"

"OK. But I'll need to take a bus or hitchhike to your place. Where do you live?"

"I live right off of Franklin Avenue, by Griffith Park. I'm a block south of Franklin."

She gave me her address, and I told her I would come find her tomorrow. She described her house as an old, beautiful three-story mansion.

"Inside the front door is a circular staircase. Take it up to the end, three storeys. There you will see a door and knock on it. That's where I live," she said. "In the peaked attic. The house is owned by a rich guy named Roy. He rents out rooms to students."

Then I paid the tab for the teas and cherry soups, and we left the Greek restaurant. She took me the few blocks up Cahuenga Boulevard to Byron's house, and we said goodbye till tomorrow. I'm sure she thought that would be the last she would see of me, as I got out of the car. Guess again, babe!

Since that time in early 1968 I have thought about our meeting and the circumstances many times. I did come find her, and we spent the day together. We talked about art, fine art, Medieval and Renaissance art, modern art, music, and poetry. I would soon find out that she was a fine poet, had published her first poem at age nineteen. During the lifetime we spent together she would be honored for her poetry, performance art, music, and filmmaking. But what intrigues me still is something else about that evening when we met.

When I was twelve years old, my dad and I were talking about art. Dad had said to me "Frankie, a lot of people think that music is the highest form of art. But I don't. I think that poetry is the highest form of art." I asked, "Why's that, Dad?" He responded, "Because the purpose of poetry is to elevate the language, to make it easier for people to express themselves in beautiful ways, whether it be for their emotions, or their perceptions, or ideas, and so forth." I never forgot that. I started writing poetry when I was sailing the world's seas, and when I was in school in Italy, travelling in Africa, and so on, several years before I met Linda.

So here I was in Los Angeles hitchhiking on a nasty, rainy night, and of all those thousands of cars passing me by at rush hour, one should stop for me, with who in it? A poet.

So we see here: a young man whose father had done his master's thesis on the poetry of Carl Sandburg and the American Civil War, who taught his son about poetry, a son who would write poetry, who gets picked up on a rainy night by a persistent, beautiful young woman poet his age. She could have kept going after the first honking, but she didn't. She honked even louder the second time and beckoned him with her arm out the car window. And they both knew about cherry soup. Linda would say forever to friends "Frank is the only guy in LA who knew about cherry soup." We would evolve quickly to become "an item.". Then partners and stay together even withstanding a couple of rough times we would need to go through, but always staying in close contact to settle our differences.

Thirty-five years after Linda and I had met, I was out to lunch with my Italian-American Roman Catholic buddy from Chicago, Tony. Sitting across from each other, I had been talking in eloquent terms about my two favorite people: Linda and my dad. When I finally throttled down (that's airplane talk, I have a commercial pilot's license), Tony looked at me straight in my eyes and said, "Ya know what, Frank, ya know what I know?" I replied, "No, Tony, what?" "What I know is, Linda was your dad's gift to you from his grave." I was stunned and silenced by what he said. I could only stare at him thoughtfully, as I weighed in my mind what he had just said. Tony knew Linda and he loved her. She was, after all, half Italian-American and gentle and kind and friendly to everybody. Tony never knew my dad except through me. What he knew about my dad was sufficient to allow him to say what he said. I could not disagree with what he said. Linda and I had another couple of decades to go with our rich and wonderful relationship—including not just one, but two marriages, no divorces, and a lot of happiness. Tony could see all of that happening ahead of time. Dear Tony, may you RIP.

And Linda has told me that our relationship was preordained. I cannot argue with that.

As our relationship developed into spring and summer, Linda decided she wanted to move to the Ocean Park–Venice neighborhood of Los Angeles. I did, too. We both got single apartments very close to each other. Here, life would be different. It was a community full of artists, students, intellectuals, filmmakers, poets, and so forth. And very close by was the sea, the wonderful Pacific Ocean, and the Santa Monica–Venice Beach. There were good places to eat on the cheap, as the clientele were not yet affluent, but working on it. Plus, one bonus Linda and I loved about living in Ocean Park, and soon Venice, was to drive from town west down Ocean Park Boulevard and going up the hill to Fourth Street just before our turn onto Third Street. At the top of the hill the view in front of us would suddenly open to show us not far away, the beach and beyond. The great and beautiful expanse of the Pacific Ocean. We always loved that view. Later on, Linda would write a powerful and moving and popular poem called "To The Pacific."

By this time, I had a car and drove back and forth from Venice into Beverly Hills to work nights at the Cedars-Sinai Hospital psychiatric ward, while waiting to start at UCLA, where they had given me a scholarship. Linda would often stop by to see me on her way to or from one of her jobs or a music gig in Hollywood.

We had a kitchen on the ward, so I would make us a couple of sandwiches and grab something to drink and meet her outside for a snack. Or some days, if I were working days, after work we would ride down Sunset Boulevard before she went to work in the evening. The first time we drove down Sunset Boulevard in my new used car I reached over to my right and took her left hand from her knee and kissed it. She liked that, and during the coming years I would do that, kiss her hand while I was driving, maybe, oh, thousands of times over the years. She never objected.

I came out to Hollywood as a stage actor, remember? By July I was fed up with what I called the lurid scene in the Hollywood entertainment industry, although I had met a lot of good people there. In the meantime, I had made contact with Wiliam Ball's great American Conservatory Theatre in San Francisco, a repertory stage group. I had decided to leave Los Angeles and head north to the city by the Bay. That evening late, after I had packed, I went over to Linda's apartment to kiss her goodbye. I told her I had an opportunity to return to the stage. She was quiet, subdued, but sweet about it, wished me luck. We said goodbye.

Looking back, I wondered if there had ever been anybody in my family, besides me, who maybe had brain fog —what was I thinking? I couldn't sleep all night. I kept thinking about Linda and how lucky I was to know her. In the morning, I went back to see her. It went like this:

"Oh, I thought you were leaving for San Francisco?"

"Uh, well, I changed my mind."

End of conversation. We went out to breakfast together. It turns out that my corrective instincts were right, time has proven that. This was still in year one of our pending long and wonderful relationship. My intuition to stay in Los Angeles would turn out to be right, for many reasons. Linda and I were beginning to have a profound influence on each other. An example of her instincts and influence on me follows:

Toward the end of that first summer Linda was preparing to go back to UCLA film school. Late one morning she asked me if I could take her to UCLA as she had a meeting there and her car was not acting right. I said "sure" and so we went to campus in my car. When we got there, she realized that we were an hour early, so she suggested that I park and we could walk across campus to an outdoor food stand and grab a bite to eat. Sounded good to me, so I parked the car. I had not been to the UCLA campus before this time. As we walked across the grass in the middle of the giant quadrangle, the center of campus surrounded by classroom buildings, we walked past a looming, magnificent building that was built in the Italian Renaissance style. The closer we got to it, the more I could only stare at its beauty in wonder, as it took me straight back to my University of Perugia days in Italy. Tears came to my eyes, and at one point I stood in front of the place, Royce Hall, and could not move. Linda saw the emotion on my face and asked me about it. I had spoken of Italy many times to her, shown her the poems I had written while in Italy, and she quickly understood the reason for my emotion.

As I recovered from the gorgeous site, we walked to the food stand, ordered something, and ate. While we were eating, she said: "Y'know, if you're gonna stay in LA, you should apply to UCLA and finish your BA degree. You're smart, and with your university background you'd get in, and probably with some scholarship money."

I had not thought of this, and I started to ponder it, because it made good sense. Linda had good ideas. Over the coming weeks I went to the Administration building on campus a couple of times to speak with one of the registrars there, a great lady named Madeline. She was impressed with my background in university education, oceanography, theatre work, and my worldwide travel.

Linda was right, I was accepted to UCLA, plus I was awarded some scholarship and grant money. I decided to major in Philosophy and European Languages, a double major. But since I had only been a California resident since January, I would have to wait until January 1969 i.e., a full year, to be fully enrolled as a California resident. In the meantime, I could, and did, audit some classes in Philosophy. I would graduate at the end of spring quarter, 1971, at the top of my class with Summa Cum Laude Honors; shortly thereafter, I was notified that I had been elected to join the prestigious academic society Phi Beta Kappa. So Linda's idea a couple of years earlier had been a good one! She would always be a good influence on me.

But getting back to 1968, our relationship was developing in ways that would always be true of us: we had each other's back. We were there for each other, no matter what. A seminal circumstance arose at UCLA for Linda that began in the fall quarter of 1968. She would be taking a film class that would require her to use a heavy Arriflex 16-millimeter camera. So she checked out the camera on loan from the film department and decided to look for a brace that would help her carry the weight of it on her shoulder. I was not aware of her search, but one afternoon at home she was looking glum. I asked her: "What's a matter? You look a little down, or something."

"Oh, I have to go to court tomorrow. I've never been to court."

"Court? You? For what?" I thought maybe it was for a traffic ticket.

"Oh, I went to the Sears in Santa Monica to see if I could find something that would help me brace the Arriflex on my shoulder, because it's heavy, and I'm going to be walking around with it. So I was in the hardware department walking around the tables of stuff, and I happened to walk by the table where the batteries are stacked. I needed some batteries too, so I grabbed a couple of them, and put them in my pullover pocket, because my hands were full of other stuff. Then I walked by the doors to go to the other side of that department, and I was arrested by two guards. They accused me of shoplifting. I wasn't shoplifting."

"I know you weren't. You wouldn't do anything like that. That crap is way beneath your dignity. What time do you have to be in court tomorrow?"

"9:00am. Why?"

"Because I'm going with you."

"Why?"

"Why? To tell the judge what happened. And to tell him that you would not do anything like that. That's why. I'm gonna tell him."

"Oh."

She didn't really know what to say. It turns out that she had never had a defender before, someone who would stick up for her. As I was getting to know her, I was learning a lot about her background as a kid and teenager. It had been a rough go for her. Very rough.

She was born in Moab, Utah to a surveyor father and an artist mother. She was their first child, and four years later her brother Jim was born. They moved to Denver when the kids were small. Her father was a jerk, and he abandoned his family when Linda was eight years old, and Jim was four. On his way out of town he told the Denver "child welfare" (an oxymoron) authorities that their mother could not support them or take care of them, which was not true. So Alberta, Linda's mom, a young woman who did not know how to defend herself, lost the kids. And the wonderful, "child welfare" authorities committed an atrocity: they put the two small kids into separate foster homes, not to see each other for years. Later on, as adults, both Linda and Jim had terrible stories to tell about having grown up in foster homes.

The next day we started early for the Santa Monica Courthouse, not far away. Linda had dressed herself well for the occasion. As young people, we could show up more casually dressed than older folks for serious occasions. Linda wore her best jeans, a cowgirl shirt with a bandana around her neck, and cowboy boots. She wore a lot of color normally, and always looked elegant. She had a great sense of style by nature, lots of color and design, and she loved chiffon scarves of many abstract designs. As she was so tall and therefore noticeable, she made it a point to look good, but not flashy.

When we got to the courthouse we sat in the hallway until the courtroom doors were opened. She had brought along one of her UCLA course books to read while waiting. But I needed to talk to her first.

"Look, Linda, when we go inside, we will walk straight up to the first pew. I will go in first, then you sit beside me on the aisle, and we'll wait for the judge to call your name. When he calls your name, you stand up and he will tell you to come stand in front of the court and face him. He will swear you in, and ask you some questions, and you tell him what you told me. And deny that you ever stole anything. And that you don't steal, period. OK?"

"OK."

I could tell she was nervous, so I held her hand.

"What are you gonna do, Frank?"

"Don't worry. At the appropriate time you'll see. It will be OK."

I hoped.

After a few minutes the judge entered the courtroom and the process started. He looked at his papers and called the first accused person up before him. Linda watched this process unfold three times, and then her name was called. She went up and stood before him, looking up at him in his perch. He swore her in, had her state her name, and he asked her a few questions. Then he read to her the accusation of shoplifting. He gave her the opportunity to tell her side of the story, which she did. He then said in a cursory way, "sure." Like he didn't believe her.

Then the judge started to read her the riot act, telling her he could put her in jail for fourteen days, and so forth. At that point I started waving my long arms into the air over my head, hard to ignore. He looked at me, then looked at Linda.

"Do you know this young man?"

"Yes, your honor, he's my friend Frank."

He looked back at me. Rather imperiously he said to me, "Do you have something you want to say, Mr. Frank?"

"Yes, Your Honor."

"Alright. Stand up and approach the bench and I will swear you in."

I did, he did, and then he asked me what I had to say.

Emphatically, I started, looking hard into his eyes.

"Your Honor, I know this young lady. I also know that she doesn't steal or shoplift, and she did not shoplift those batteries at Sears. Stealing is beneath her dignity. She is a very honest person, and I know that."

I was forceful, and he looked me straight in the eyes while I was talking. When I finished, he waited a few seconds, then said to me:

"Alright, here's what I can do. Mr. Frank, this young lady I am going to remand into your custody. Do you know what that means?"

"Yes, I do, Your Honor. She will be my responsibility."

"Yes, and it also means that if either one of you get out of line and end up back in this court, I will put you both in jail for fourteen days. How's that, Mr. Frank?"

"That's fine, Your Honor. Neither one of us will get into trouble. That's fine with me."

"OK, then, both of you step over to your left, and sign a paper the bailiff has there for you to sign, and then you're dismissed."

"Thank you, Your Honor."

And that was it.

And that episode had seminal and deep meaning to both of us over the coming years. Because it was the first time that Linda had someone who would go out on a limb and stick up for her, defend her, believing she was telling the truth. That ethos between us would never change over the next five and one-half decades. I would always "have her back". And true to her good nature and sense of loyalty, she would always have my back. We believed in each other.

Over the coming years as we grew to know and love each other more, and to have each other's back, and take care of each other, she would come to call me her Champion, or her Rock, or because of my background, her Renaissance Man. But I would come to call her my Anchor, because what I loved most in my life was coming home to her, or watching her walk down our neighborhood streets as she came home to me.

Our lives went on together for five and one-half decades; more details about Linda's life are covered elsewhere in this book. Before Covid hit humanity in 2019–2020, Linda had told me she wanted the two of us to do a book of poetry together. She wanted people to know about my poetry, because she loved my poetry as

I loved hers. But she also wanted people to know about us. She was the public figure, prominent in four arts for over forty years. I was the quiet one behind the scenes, and she called me her audience cheerleader . . . or "clacker"!

We both had lived extraordinary lives before we met. Linda had been an Honors Student at University of Colorado, Boulder, and a Homecoming Queen. She published her first poem at age nineteen in Southern California. She had done some modeling and TV and film work in Los Angeles as an actress and was hired twice as a musician and singer by the USO to travel to Asia during the Vietnam War. She visited Japan, South Korea, Thailand, and South Vietnam twice. When I met her, she was studying filmmaking at UCLA, where she graduated as an Honors Student; her student film was awarded First Prize out of fifty films. She did not come from money and was completely self-supporting since leaving her abusive home at age nineteen and on through her university years. She would over time become prominent in film, music, performance art, and poetry. Linda performed in venues across North America, Europe, and Africa, listed elsewhere in this book. Among her stage performances were two world tours with the famous Alice Cooper's Nightmare and Nightmare Returns in the late 1980s. The City of Los Angeles would name her as one of very few Poetry Divas for her fine poetic work.

My travels and new life out of Ohio had begun a few years before I met Linda, when I got hurt as a football lineman at Ohio State University. I graduated from high school at age seventeen and showed up in Columbus to join the OSU team on a football scholarship in August 1960, at age seventeen, six and one-half feet tall, and weighing only 217 pounds. Coach Woody Hayes had told my dad, "Don't worry, Mr. Lutz, we'll put thirty pounds on Frank his first year here." And that they did.

When I got the ankle injury and couldn't walk well for a few months, I got "redshirted" for a year. I had always wanted a European education, so I left home in Ohio in the winter, went to Florida for a few months where I worked as a lifeguard in Fort Lauderdale, and worked in the summer for a few months at the Woods Hole, Massachusetts Oceanographic Institution. Each summer they hired a few students to train in oceanography and/or crew work. I was hired to work on the famous oceanographic ship the RV (Research Vessel) Atlantis, a ketch-rigged two-master, 146 feet long, built in Denmark in 1931. After sailing the North Atlantic and the Caribbean for the summer, at the end of August 1962 I left for Paris to begin studies at the Sorbonne and their affiliate French language institute.

The next spring I returned to Ohio to play Spring Football, but I kept thinking about Europe. At the end of the season, and when the academic quarter was over, I told my Dad I was finished playing football, much as I loved the sport. He was disappointed, as he saw athletics as a way for me to get a college education for free. But I wanted to return to Europe, to study at the University of Perugia, Italy, north of Rome. Dad had been an athlete and a scholar, so he understood my desire for academia.

At about that time, the Woods Hole Oceanographic Institution called me and asked me if I would like to sail with them to the Indian Ocean, Africa, India, and parts east around the world. Of course, I said "yes" and Italy would have to wait. So for the next six months I would be on a new ship, the RV Atlantis II, built in Denmark and commissioned at the beginning of 1963. What an adventure this would turn out to be!

It would be just a few short years, and many adventures, before I would find myself on the street at night in a winter rain in West Hollywood. In between oceanography and universities in Europe, I had by accident fallen into theatre acting in community venues in Ohio, including Antioch College Summer Theatre in Yellow Springs, Ohio, and some work off-Broadway in New York City. In August of 1967 at Antioch, I was on stage in the play *The Balcony* by Jean Genet, the great French playwright. In the audience was the man who would bring me out to Hollywood, the aforementioned Byron, who I did not know at the time. After the play he introduced himself to me and told me he could get me work in Hollywood. So, in January 1968, I drove cross-country to Los Angeles.

Shortly after arriving in Los Angles, my life with Linda began. It was wonderful, and full of more spectacular accomplishments for both of us. Later, after Linda graduated from UCLA as an Honors Graduate, and was becoming well known for her accomplishments in four arts, at the same time I would go on to graduate from UCLA with Honors as a Summa Cum Laude and would be inducted into Phi Beta Kappa honors society. I became a Council M ember in the UCLA Center for Medieval and Renaissance Studies. I also became a Commercial Pilot and Flight Instructor. Our lives together were filled with great events and a lot of love.

WHO WAS SHE?

Who was this girl,
this young woman
who picked me up
on a cold winter night
in 1968?
Rain, wind, cold
on the streets and sidewalks
of Hollywood.
My jacket over my head,
cars speeding by me
on Sunset Boulevard,
honking, honking.
And then a different honk
close behind me,
but I did not turn to look.
So she honked again,
Louder, longer,
And I turned,
saw her long arm
reaching out the
passenger window,
beckoning me
to come.
I ran, looked in,
saw a tall,
beautiful young woman
my age.
"Come on, get in,
it's raining!" she told me.
Inside her car
I looked at her and said,
"Hi, my name's Frank.
What's yours?"

IT ALL BEGAN WITH CHERRY SOUP

"Linda."
Next, I thought, next . . .
"Wanna stop and have some coffee?"
"No," she said,
"But I'll stop and have
some tea and cherry soup
with you."
"Well, OK, cool!" I said.
I knew cherry soup
from when I worked
on a farm in Denmark
between semesters
at universities
I was attending in Europe.
We stopped at a Greek restaurant
in Hollywood
where we had our
tea and cherry soup,
and talked.
The next day I hitchhiked
across town again,
this time
to see her
and take a walk,
go to lunch,
hike in Griffith Park.
That was it!
Next thing I knew,
the calendar
kept changing.
Calendars do that.
Day after day,
year after year
for fifty-five years.
Then she got sick,

PART II

really sick.
I had saved her
our first year together
from a false
criminal charge
against her.
She didn't know how
to defend herself.
I told the judge forcefully
that I knew her,
who she was,
her high degree of integrity,
and that I knew
she would not do
what she was
accused of doing,
it was beneath
her dignity.
He believed me,
remanded her to
my custody,
let her off the hook.
Later on we would move
to Venice together,
buy a house together,
go to UCLA together,
start a business together,
be each other's
support system,
her in the arts,
me in academia,
stay together,
travel the world together,
hold hands together,
look in each other's eyes,

and love each other,
together.
Now we would fight
for her survival together.
But alas, we would not win
this battle together.
Our pitiful medical industry
for fifty years-plus
has had neither the
competence nor the brains,
despite our money,
to figure out
a cure
for pancreatic cancer.
And so
the Love of my Life,
the brilliant and beautiful
and gentle woman
who I married and adored,
died in the early dawn
of a September morning in 2022
did go away
with my heart in her
gentle hands.
Linda J. Albertano,
The Best Person
I ever met.

MY LOVELY WORDSMITH

It's remarkable
to me
when I think back
five and one-half
decades ago
that she would
pick me up
in her '53 Mercury Coupe
on a cold and rainy evening,
the kind of things
the kids did back then
to help each other,
and that Linda and I would
stay together
for five and one-half decades,
and love each other
more each year,
each year,
each year,
until the day
she left this Earth.
But we knew
our love
for each other
would go on and on,
and it does.
Linda more recently
in our years together
told me,
"Frank, it was
Preordained,"
as she remarked
on how strongly

we felt about
each other.
We were alike
and unalike.
This sentiment
was felt
and believed
by me, too.
Shortly in our
knowing each other
back then,
I would find out
she was a poet.
I was a poet too,
but it would be
years
before I told
her that,
as I never wanted
her to think
that I might
compete
with her
for recognition.
She found out
anyway.
She had discovered
and read
my thick portfolio
of poems.
I had been writing
poetry
since I had been
travelling around
the world on

PART II

oceanographic ships,
a young student scientist,
stopping in places
like Africa, India,
islands in the
far oceans,
or studying
in universities
in Europe.
Over time, of course,
Linda would present
her poetry
and performance art
all across America
and on three
continents.
She would become
recognized
and acclaimed
for her work in poetry,
performance art,
music and film.
Sometime before Covid
she said to me,
"Hankie, I want us
to publish a book
of poetry together.
I love your poems."
I said, "You love
my poems?
Why?"
She looked at me
with her usual
sweet face, and said,
"Because they

make people cry."
I didn't know
what to say.
Then Covid hit,
and then the world
seemed to stop
for a while.
After it was
pretty much over,
on April 7, 2022
Linda woke up
that morning
and said to me
"Hankie, I feel
a lump
in my tummy.
I think
we should go
to the doctor."
I replied,
"Absolutely."
And we went.
The news
was not good.
It was all about
her pancreas.
During the
next five months,
we tried everything
available in conventional
and alternative medicine.
To no avail.
We got married
for the second time
on Tuesday, September 6,

PART II

and on Tuesday, September 13
my dear sweet Linda,
Love of my Life,
passed away
at 4:40 in the morning.
Now all three
of the people
I loved most—
Mom, Dad, and Linda,
were all gone
from Mother Earth.
But it is not over.
After she passed,
I knew that she would be
as desperate
to talk to me,
as I would be
to talk to her.
And so I went
on yet another
long journey
of discovery.
I needed to study
Afterlife communications,
with scientists, medical people,
researchers, Medium practitioners,
people who have had
Near Death Experiences,
and people who have had
the sublime experience
of talking with
their departed loved ones.
I have also read more than
fifty-seven books
on the subjects, starting with

quantum mechanics science.
Truth be told,
I can now communicate
with my Linda, almost
on a daily basis.
Some of you
will understand this,
some of you will not
but will want to understand it,
and some of you
will treat what I say
with skepticism.
I am happy to pass
onto you all anything
I can to help you.
Linda would have
it no other way.
And believe me,
if I were not to
help you,
I would hear it
from
Linda.

PART II

THE LOVE ACHE

I can't take her anywhere
anymore.
Not out to eat
at her favorite places,
nor to the movies,
nor to the opera,
nor on short trips
like to Santa Barbara,
nor to New York City;
nor to Europe,
nor to Africa,
nor back to Rome '
so I can finish
my Vatican project.
I can't even hold her hand anymore.
Before Covid hit
three years ago
we were planning Rome.
Then that plague
infected the world.
But as the world-wide infection
was subsiding,
in April of this year 2022,
Linda discovered a lump
in her tummy.
Off to the doctors
and the limits they gave her,
no surgery, no radiation,
only chemotherapy.
And so—she elected not
to suffer incapacitated
if these were to be her
last months with us

who she loved, and who loved her.
There, then started our
six-month journey
with the alternative care folks,
in Mexico and Canada and here.
But in August she was feeling uneasy,
to the extent that she told me
"Hankie, I might not make it,
I might die."
To which I cried out
"No, Linda, you can't die!
I would rather die,
than to see you die!"
To which she cried back
with wide-open eyes,
"No, Frank, no—
I could not survive without you.
I would not know what to do!"
I had no response to that,
and only comforted her.
Just before midnight,
on Friday evening, September 2nd,
she was having pains in her tummy,
more than usual.
I took her to UCLA Hospital,
where they admitted her
and made her comfortable,
and took her into a nice room.
This would be her last place to be alive.
We loved each more than words can express,
so on Tuesday afternoon, September 6th,
we got married—for the second time!
But that's a story for another time.
During the week that followed
she worked in the morning constantly

on her computer,
typing new poems and new ideas
for new shows, into September,
October, November—
She was not giving up!
Then on Saturday, Sunday, Monday,
I could tell something different
was happening.
She was getting weaker,
sleeping more,
not working so much
on her beloved computer.
I was exhausted Monday evening
from not eating, not sleeping.
I had tried to sleep
in a very uncomfortable chair
by her bed, the night before,
but to no avail.
So at about 8:30pm
I kissed her on her sleeping head
and went home,
fell asleep in my clothes.
At 4:45am I received a call:
"Mr. Lutz, this is UCLA Hospital
calling you.
I am very sorry to tell you
that your dear wife Linda
has passed away this morning,
at 4:40am . . ."
I had no idea
that her end was so near.
In a daze I drove back to
her room.
She was at peace,
beautiful, always beautiful.

I kissed her on her forehead
as she lay in her bed.
then I sat in the chair by her bed,
and took her hand in mine,
and I spoke to her:
"Linda, I will always love you, I will love you forever. And as Dante followed Virgil when Virgil beckoned him, when you see my time is near, beckon me like Virgil beckoned Dante, and I will follow you. And I will find you again, my Love."
That would be the last time I will see her,
the last time I will hold her hand, until . . .

IN MEMORIAM

She lit up the stages she visited with profusions of words that sparkled in the air, her mellifluous voice giving tonic beauty to each syllable of her works. She loved life and poetry and especially us, we the people. Her lines of words will motivate and melt forever the hearts of those of us who read them, and at times help us laugh with joy. She was and will remain Linda J. Albertano, Poetry Diva.

—*Frank Lutz*

PART III
POEMS BY LINDA J. ALBERTANO

IT ALL BEGAN WITH CHERRY SOUP

44

REINCARNATION

Kora, didn't I meet you in
a previous lifetime? And
aren't you more than a musical
creature dressed in
skin and cowrie shells? I've seen
your supernatural harp-strings
aim missiles of crisp sound
at our feet
forcing us to dance! (willing
or not).

You play
with matches near our frail and
fatal happiness, singeing
us from root-of-hair to
tap-of-toe. One
day you'll burn us down to
red-eyed cinders.

Kora, are you the great-ancestor of
all music? Because I hear tones Celtic,
Gregorian, Bach and Beethoven-like
roll from your stately
strings. In a previous life, you've sent
syncopated glory and Dixieland marching
down the ragtime streets in
our veins.
And in your wild
wave-forms dwells a velvet-voiced
legend from Memphis, Tennessee.

IT ALL BEGAN WITH CHERRY SOUP

Kora, the first time I heard
you, you bit
me with the bad juju. You grabbed
me by the hair and dragged
me into the deep
end. You flattened
me with cascade after crescendo of
celestial sound.
I learned to worship in the opulent
church of your holy
exuberance. Your sacred
music lines the ears of
God with extravagant
notes of grace.
You've caused hosts of
angels to weep. Their
fragile tears
burst into fireworks of sound
like a thousand tiny
goblets dashed against a
fireplace of jubilation!

Kora, I'm sure we've met before. I
recognize you in the whoop and
holler of banjos going. I've seen you
explode in the shake and
shimmy of every soulful, celebratory
stomp there is. I've met you in
the pop and snap of
rock and roll, in the flash
of midnight jazz. I hear
your Hallelujah Chorus in
the songs of the Georgia Sea
Islands and in every gospel choir

known to exist. They
daily sing your praises to
deities public and
powerful. And you
sass us back in
your native tongue!

By the way, didn't you and
your fingerpicking, back-beat rhythms
buddy up to
Robert Johnson and
Skip James?
Weren't you high-steppin' it
with Bessie Smith
and Billie Holliday?
Haven't you been found
in the DNA
of Ray Charles? Mingus? Coltrane?
and Miles Davis?
I even heard
you once
had an address in the
funky part of
Motown, as well!

Kora. We've met before. I'm sure
we have. We've
known you
in lustrous lifetimes
past. I've
witnessed the very
gods bend to the snap
and ring of your
irresistible strings.

Kora,
We've known you. In all
your famous forms. You're
disguised as calabash and
simple fishing line in
<u>this</u> incarnation. But you're
far more than a thing of skin.
And shell could ever be.

Kora.

I know we've met. Yes!
Yes. Yes.

I remember now . . .

In lustrous lifetimes past.

Kora.

I <u>know</u> we've met before.

I never forget a face.

Kora.

PARTY GIRL

The Party Girl is moving very slowly.
She is shaped like a broken toothpick.
She feels like a railroad tie.
Her head is knotted in a rag.
Her insides are nailed to the ground.
She's ingested not a morsel in three weeks.
She is fainting and having visions.

Wild geese are singing in her cells.

The Party Girl is on death row.
She is living on air and water.
The date of her last meal is the 18th day of April.
Cops come and drag her away.
He who chars her spirit with his smallest
sneer is chewing on her heart.

He stabs it with a forked tongue.

The Party Girl is fasting and meditating.
She prays for his roasted soul.
She prays for her own.
She prays for guidance.

No answers come.

The Party Girl wears a blue shirt under striped overalls.
She puts her shoulders in the harness every day.
She types and files and keeps the books at night.
She resurrects the corpse of desire only in her mind.
Work and more work.

She is becoming a dull boy.

The Party Girl is thin and wan.
Twenty-three days and counting.
Nothing but water pure has passed her lips.
She is thirty pounds smaller.
It looks like Andersonville Prison in the mirror.
The Day of the Dead.
He who electrocutes her happiness with his slightest smirk
decides it must be drugs.

He sucks long and hard on his hash pipe.

The Party Girl is wearing black.
She is laying lilies on the grave of hope.
She is emaciated with grief.
She remembers how He who drove screws into the thumbs
of her joy smiled when she screamed.

She places one last lily.

The Party Girl is writing in an empty ledger.
Dark words bleed through white pages like ugly
tattoos from beneath her skin.
"In the beginning angels sang behind his every breath,"
she writes. The plot disintegrates from there.
The story stinks of decay.

She buries it in a shallow ditch.

The Party Girl is going home.
She corks the sad champagne.
She packs the shriveled balloons in a leather valise.
She is walking away from Rio.
She hears wild geese fly past her ears as she goes.
She knows she will never return.

She grows tiny on the horizon of his memory.

Then the Party Girl completely disappears.

IF . . . IT'S NOIR.

If Jean-Paul Belmondo is rubbing his lower lip with his thumb and Jean Seberg is "Breathless," it's noir.

If the seams in her silk stockings run all the way from her black garter belt to deep inside her high heels, it's noir.

If she's a silhouette in a calf-length coat against a mood of swirling fog, it's noir.

If you find her ringside, staining an unfiltered camel with her fire-engine lips while her dough—all of it—is riding on an overmatched boxer defending against a cacophony of blows, it's noir.

If your detective, rather than your breakfast, is hard boiled, it's noir.

STRIKE

The Statue of Liberty is
weeping. Long
has she lifted her welcoming
torch for the tired, the
poor, and all the others
yearning for one
honeyed breath of freedom.
Now she's seen democracy's
golden door slammed hard
on their weary fingers. What
will she say? Look
up! Look up!

Don't let them crush you, my lovely
native-born, whose ancestors
spoke in the tongue of the
Algonquin and in that of the
Zapoteca and in the
languages of all the Americas. Don't
let them crush your children, my sweet
and earthy immigrants who arrived
here from the far-flung
lands of the Celts, the Franks, the
Anglo-Saxons, and of the Indo-Europeans.
Nor you, whose mothers came
speaking Cantonese or Japanese. Yoruba,
Wolof, Malinke. The silken sounds of Arabia. Or
Russian and the Slavic tongues, brilliant
as chips of ice melting in the air!

My Rainbow Warriors, you are all
here! With the noble sons and daughters of
the Islands. You've come with

dreams shining as
the seas that brought you. Of
living in friendship together eternal as
the sun is bright and long as
the rivers shall run.
From the green and sacred
forests of the Seneca to the
luminous wind-ruffled waves of Chief
Seattle, we native-born and
foreign-born have bent our backs as
though into the long oars of
a magnificent ship. And ours are
the labors that have created one
nation for all! Not one nation
for some. But one nation
for all.

And those who labor longest and
hardest among us
bring comforts, large and
small
into our lives. Without
which, all the world would be
in chaos. Your labors bring the
greatest good to the
largest number!

World without grocery workers . . .
bitter and barren.
World without bus drivers . . .
bitter and barren.
World without truckers . . .
bitter and barren.
Food servers, sanitation workers, janitors . . .

We need you! Desperately. You've
added more value to
our lives than all the golf-playing
CEOs on the planet ever could!

We cherish you! And your families!! We
pray for your good health and for the righteous
and equitable fruits you deserve to harvest
when you've retired from service. We're
here to stand with you!
To see that you receive more than
a pocket watch and a Christmas ham at the
end of your labors. We know that if we
let them rob you today, they'll come
to rob us tomorrow.

Look up!
The Statue of Liberty is standing
even taller. Her lamp burns
more brightly for you!

Look up!
We're standing shoulder-to-shoulder. And
look how brightly the
lamp of justice
is shining.

Look up!
We're standing shoulder-to-shoulder.

Look up! Look up.

WOMEN WITHOUT MEN

Women Without Men!
They stalk the lonely streets
at night.
Professional Women!
Brain surgeons.
Architects.
Certified Public Accountants.
Women who know how
to balance a checkbook!

Meanwhile . . .
Scores of tormented men
commit suicide
for sheer want of a quiet woman,
pliant as a hammock,
waiting
to be fallen into.

You'd think
the Women Without Men
would wise up.
You'd think they'd shut up.

But they long for the day
when they will be
White Collar Criminals
reaping a buck
for every fifty cents
that leaks out in the other direction!

Who will have to Listen Good
then? they query.

PART III

They want quiet men,
pliant as hammocks
waiting . . .
    waiting . . .
        waiting . . .

to be fallen into.

SABOTAGE

Now the news has hit the streets—our love is in danger.
Watch out for impeccable strangers.
That insidious female with the pink corsage
might be a case of sabotage.

Some inner pinball signals "tilt" when she asks you for a light . . .
so cool and nonchalant, you don't need to be too bright
to see the pieces fall together in that sinister collage
of double cross and sabotage.

That woman is a slimy operator
doing what I knew she would,
but you've been a willing collaborator, honey,
you're up to no good.

Now you've delivered all our secrets
and you've tightened up the noose.
You've wired me like a light bulb and you're leaning on the juice.
Will they find me in the trunk of a derelict Dodge?
—a victim of love and sabotage.

Oh, love and sabotage.

THE DEATH OF KONG

I was his wife. He
held me with his big
hands, quiet
like the tops of coconut
trees on a breathless
day. I was tender
pudding melting
in the palms of God.
Lick me clean again!
His death let the air out
of my life.

When I think of him steel
doors close
on the fingers of my womb.
Memory is the steam
roller parked
on my chest. His bad self
whispers dirty
secrets to my soul. Unpaid
promises stabbed
like bills on the spike
of my heart.

Breakfast at midnight. Fresh
eggs and fish. Beautiful
bananas!

Think. After all
these years I still
hold his taste in my empty
mouth. Odd
how he spent his last

days pounding a lunatic SOS
on his chest bone
and stuffing
our love into a bare
coffin. I stopped hearing
his music. Still.
He could always
make me laugh. How
long has it been since
I heard that sound?

Oh. I wish
I could remember
how to be a woman
again. Nowadays I forget
which of us is
gone.

I was his wife. Buried
alive.

FREUD'S SLIPPER SHUFFLE

One night I dreamed I was a man.

I woke up & found Freud sitting by my bed.
He was wearing the slippers
my mother bought him. Those
blue terry scuffs with the open heel?

He really loves those slippers! He wears them
to every tieless, sockless occasion he can
think of.

Like to Nick the Greek's for tiny little cocktail
onions. Or to Sardi's for
beer & pig's feet!

But about that dream.

Freud asked me what I thought it meant.
I said I didn't know,
but I dreamt long ago, I was a dime store
detective rescuing a
<u>blonde</u> from hideous grinning
death. I looked a lot like
Bogey. She was <u>real</u> grateful. She had
<u>lips</u> like overripe tomatoes. I could hardly
wait to sink my teeth into her.

Boy! Imagine my
surprise when I
woke up & found out I was
<u>nothing</u>! but a skinny little girl in a pink
flannel sleeping suit with a trapdoor bottom!

I dunno what to think about the 5 o'clock
shadow, though . . . Maybe
I should run for president? And

is Bogey <u>really</u> a universal symbol
in the collective unconscious?

INGOT

Oh no!

This leaden weightedness, density
of my body lies
crumpled, thrown away
like gum wrapper of twisted
ingot (not
of tinfoil). Say I
didn't do it!

The solid
tonnage of atmosphere
pins
me to the floor
(no).

Don't leave me!
My eyes are hot.

I am
a man who's crushed
a woman with
his own two hands (no, no,
say I didn't do it).
So sturdy were the bones
of her face
they refused
to turn into pulp until long,
long after my taste for her
blood had been lost (oh no),
and these arms

had become mechanical
things whose twin pumpings
I could only stand and watch.

I could only
stand and watch,
the full of it
caught deep in my throat.

Lord! And this to the woman
I loved. No!

Oh no.

I "LIKE" YOUR DOPPELGANGER!

Some say that Hitler's doubles were all alike. At least the one they found in the bunker with Eva Braun.

Some say he fooled the Russian army for 3 whole days. But, NO . . . despite his lopsided hairdo and absurdly parsimonious upper lip décor.

Some say he was too damned short to be the absolute McCoy. Plus . . . suicide with a bullet planted precisely between those eyebrows? With zero powder burns to show for it?? Exactly.

Some say their devious escapee had simply hopped a willing submarine and chunneled under the Atlantic (disgorging in Buenos Aires).

Would that other odious despots should but stow away on errant U-boats and live their last irrelevant decades as addled gauchos bellowing self-praise to startled longhorns on the Argentine Pampas!

One eternal day, they . . . and we . . . will be as fine silt drifting between Indianapolis and the rings of Saturn.

In that singular spit of time we shall all, quite bravely and equitably, be nothing . . . but persistently, unavoidably, inexorably, undeniably, irrevocably and utterly   alike.

(we are all   nothing   but   alike)

PROGRESS

I dunno. Where
did it all start?
We shoulda built a barricade
against all this inventive
intellect.
        Phonograph records?
                Teletype machines?
                        Smart Phones?

Impale their metal carcasses on flame-
hardened stakes! Where
was Dracula
when we needed him?

I see Madame Curie—lit
from within by radio-
active fireflies—sifting
through mountains of pitchblende
for the stuff of the 10th
dimension!
        Nuclear Submarines?
                Three Mile Island?
                      Neutron Bombs?

I see Gibson Girl touch
tip of paintbrush to lip to form
point perfect. Pandora
putting faces on the luminous
dials of watches. Oh, radium,
radium! When
did your kiss become
cancer?

PART III

Perhaps
Inquisitors were correct when
They quashed Galileo
And Copernicus for dangerous
thought.
Attack Drones?
Artificial intelligence?
                      Pandemic Virology?

Humankind grunts, "must monkey
with gears of doom."
At least jam
scissors of science into electrical
outlets of infinity.

Karl Marx said machines would free
the enslaved. We could loll
forever in the arms of
Philosophy.

Hah!

Each new time-
saving instrument only speeds
the revolutions of our helpless labors.

Question:
If Dolphins had prehensile
thumbs
and the wheel, would
<u>they</u> have come
to this?

We're a blur
on the turn-
table of time. Spinning
into butter. Spinning
into white illumination. Is <u>that</u>
what is meant by
Nirvana? Oh,
well. Even intelligent
toddlers will soon have
the bomb.

1000 light-
years away may
the sight of our disintegrating
Super Nova instruct other
advanced civilizations.

There's such a thing
as being too
damned smart for your own damned
good.

We're <u>brilliant</u> insects. I only hope
our fossils can fuel alien
spacecraft
for millennia to come!

OF THE EARTH

Deep in the earth a pickaxe arcs through
atmosphere like a meditation beyond the caprice
of being . . . a sparkle of stars on the tongues
of believers.

Each pock of the pick ignites a dazzle
of saline shards . . . lit from the utmost reach
of time to be resurrected in midnight cylinders
of blue.

Upon which unnumbered umbrellas
shield children from an elaborate universe
as they spill shimmers of quiet points behind
their shoes.

Then aboard boxcars, all glide seamlessly under
the big dipper for destinations exotic
and mundane.

Someone sips a margarita.
Someone seasons a steak.
Someone kisses the tears from a
toddler's cheek

And in the dark, from great dunes surrounding
the lake, salt floats upward on rivulets
of white air . . . penitent supplications whispered
into the thick and final dome
of night.

MAJESTIC LANDFILL

In order to cut carbon, they'll soon be serving grubs and mealworms on intercontinental flights.

If insects can't out-crawl, out-skitter or outrun extinction, can birds or bipeds be far behind?

At least we've halted salting the sea with plastic straws.

But some of the juices that feed our Teslas are wrung from fire-breathing plants.

And not the kind of greenery squeezed from the flaming orange orb that incrementally boils us in our own sweat, either.

O, diminutive human beings . . . are we the only species stuck on self-destruct?

Lemmings lunge after their leaders over cliffs. Yet lemmings abound. Hope in a storm of despair?

A modern bard foretold this catastrophe when he sang,
"It's the Slow Consumption killing us by degrees."

Sing, people! Sing! Whilst our stumpy legs carry us to the eternal landfill in the sky.

Sing!

CHRISTOPHER COLUMBUS TRANSCONTINENTAL HIGHWAY

500 years ago, when C. Columbus first set pointy
foot on the eastern shores of heaven, how was he to know they'd give a transcontinental highway his name one day, and that it'd stretch all the way from Jacksonville, Florida to Lincoln Blvd. in Santa Monica, CA?

And if he were still on his pins, would he ride
shotgun down route 10 in a pink T-bird with black and silver fins driven by a conquistador pal? Would they hand over twenty simoleons to park on the tarmac at Venice Beach?

And when they ran across the souls of Jim
Morrison and Orson Welles would they stroll
the boardwalk together sharing stashes and
snagging sunglasses for the sake of ogling Botticelli's bikinied babes baking on the sand?

Would they meet a biker named Spike,
and would he offer to guide them to Marilyn
Monroe's hallowed Memorial Park ashes?

And on the way would a goofball with a pistol
relieve them of their T-bird at a stop sign?

Yep.

500 years ago, Christopher C. told Isabella
he could take paradise with 50 armed men.
How was he to know they'd name a transcontinental highway after him? And that the 50 armed guys would still be riding on it.

Still looking to take something from someone.

Anyone.

TWINKIE DEFENSE

Somewhere in San Francisco
someone is having a twinkie
and deep-fried cheetos
for breakfast.
Later in the day
someone will shoot the mayor.
Someone will not be held responsible.

Somewhere in East LA
someone is having a breakfast
of goat's milk yogurt, wheat germ,
blackstrap molasses, and alfalfa sprouts.
No matter <u>what</u> happens
later in the day
someone <u>will</u> be held responsible.

Somewhere in San Diego
someone is having a cigarette
for breakfast
with a cappuccino
and a jelly croissant.
But someone is not responsible.
Someone will not be held responsible.

Somewhere way South of the border
someone who's spent a lifetime
harvesting sugar cane, coffee, and tobacco
for someone in San Fransisco
and someone in San Diego

is having a particularly
medieval experience.
And is held responsible.
Responsible! Responsible!

Someone is held entirely
responsible.

LOOK IN THE MIRROR

Dissent is the soul of democracy!
Who usually does it?
Now debate is labeled treason?
Go look in the mirror.

Injustice upon injustice!
Who usually does it?
Jail'em without naming the crime?
Go look in the mirror.

Billions of dollars for war!
Who usually does it?
But not a penny to spare for peace?
Go look in the mirror.

Shred treaties like Pentagon records!
Who usually does it?
Terror is the price of Empire.
Go look in the mirror.

Sell weapons of war to the world!
Who usually does it?
Anthrax in the mail?
Go look in the mirror.

Kurds or Native Americans?
Who usually does it?
Eliminate inconvenient populations.
Go look in the mirror.

Soldiers pay with their bodies!
Who usually does it?
While our leaders drink their blood.
Go look in the mirror.

Friendly fire, collateral damage!
Who usually does it?
Civilians stacked in the streets.
Go look in the mirror.

Hiroshima, Nagasaki!
Who usually does it?
Weapons of mass destruction.
Go look in the mirror.

Support brutal regimes.
Who usually does it?
Ask the Shah of Iran.
Ask Pinochet.
Ask Noriega.
Ask Duvalier.
Ask Saddam.
Ask Netanyahu.
Ask the Saudis.
And then, if you still can,
go!

Go look in the mirror!

NIGHT STALKING ARMADILLO

Trust me.

I sped from NASA at a rate of 7 corpuscle-crushing gravities for you
wearing an adult diaper with a pair of pistols strapped to my hips.

Ah, hahahahaha!
You're #1 on my thrill list, Babe.

Trust me.

For purposes of National Security, I gotta hold you in extra-sensory confinement. Ooooo.
You throttle my thrusters. Bad (!)

Trust me.

I must execute an extensive exploration of your top-secret mystery parts. All this probing.
Are Martians at the controls here? Yet, no
one expects the Inquisition.

It won't be long now. Oooops . . .
It was an accident! Just cleaning my drone,
Hon, when it went off.

Sorry.

You shoulda stood your ground!

Trust me.

NO HOLDS BARRED

Sitting in a coffee house
dreaming about love
while the jets we bought and paid for
scream up above . . .
sweating on the docks,
thinking, "What's it all for?"
Loading up guns
bound for Third World War.
No holds barred.

Lazy little country . . .
who's gonna con'em
into lunching on bullets
with our names on'em?
We'd grind your babies
into sausage go the hideous rumors,
just to keep the world safe
for conscientious consumers.
No holds barred.

It takes a stack o' Latin peasants
to keep our corporations fed,
but we feel real sad
when the body count is read.
Who could call us apathetic
with our perfect sympathies?
Of course, we might avert our eyes
while they kill you by degrees.
No holds barred.

Barnes & Noble
Presents
Open Mic Night

Featuring
LINDA ALBERTANO

poetry reading
Fri., March 31st
7:00 p.m.

NERO AT THE BARBEQUE

Rome is burning.
Rome is burning again.
It's 2,000 years later
and Rome is still burning.

Nero picks up his bow.
He plays "Fiddler on the Roof."
He plays "You don't miss your water
'til the well runs dry."
He plays "So sad to see
good love go bad."

A crowd gathers.
Across the street, a jackhammer
launches an assault on their reverie.
The Supreme Court is supervising
a demolition. The destruction
of the foundation of civil liberties
built in decades past.

Oh they'd love to turn the Bill of Rights
into a HUD project.
Tear it down. Angels Flight.
Put in a parking lot.
A shopping mall.
Somebody's gonna make some dough.

A lone guy objects.
A couple of grey-suited lawyers
grab him and pin his arms down.
Nero plays while the Supreme Court
delivers blows to the stomach of justice.

PART III

"You really got a hold on me, baby,
you really got a hold on me."
The crowd ignores the scuffle.
They figure it has nothing to do with them.
Nero wails into a screaming round of "Shimmy,
Shimmy, Koko Bop" that would scare the sneakers
off of Little Anthony.
Folks flip quarters into Nero's hat and move on.

Nearby, in the halls of state, Pontius Pilate sites
at a chess board with the mayor of the Crips. Or is it
the Bloods?
The president of the United States is keeping score.
The law is not about justice.

A window opens onto the street.
A violin version of "Shake it up, baby" floats
into the room. Pilate is annoyed.
The jackhammer racket of civil rights being ground
into flour is spoiling his concentration.
A homeboy in a T-shirt and a durag moves his black
knight to Pico and Fairfax. Check! Buildings flame
into the darkness as cheerfully as fireworks
on the Fourth of July.

The President flips a score card. Points for the
Homies. This time the while king is under siege.
No video cameras to document his bones being beaten
into pulp inside the bag of his skin.
Hmm.
It looks bad for the heads of state.

The chief of police decides to make a move.
He heads for high ground.
He splits.

He says, "I'm ready.
I'm all set. For this
or any other crisis.
See ya later, Jack."
Then he gets outta town.
Him and the ass he rode in on.
Police cars sit baffled on the black and white squares
of the playing board. Or is it the city?
Like abandoned pawns.

Because the law is not about justice.
The law alone
does not protect or serve.
The law is a game, like chess.
To the victors belong the spoils.
The scorekeeper makes up the rules.
Get a better umpire
or, one, two, three.
Burn, baby, burn.

Nero scratches maniacally
on his axe. "Wake up,
Little Susie, Wake up!"

Pontius Pilate stares with disbelief
at the chess board.
He's angry. "Wild Thing."
He crosses the floor
and slams the window down.
"You make my heart sing."
He stomps off
to the washroom.
The hands of the past are rubbing themselves raw.
But nothing comes clean.

History keeps unfolding
cranky and indignant
like Mussolini
waking after a nap.
Nero fiddles,
"I'm gonna wait
for the midnight hour."
Burn, baby, burn.

The law is not about justice.
Rome is burning again.
The law is a game like cowboys
and Indians. Like Spaniards
and Aztecs.

It's 2,000 years later
and Rome is still burning.
The law is a game and the ones
with the most guys or the biggest guns
get to be the winners.

Burn, baby, burn!

The hands of the past are rubbing
themselves raw.

But nothing . . . comes clean.

Burn!

FRIENDLY FIRE

The Statue of Liberty is
grieving. She has seen enough
purple majesty covered with
white crosses to
overwhelm
the book of the dead. She is weeping
bullets
stamped "made in the USA"
like ones left in the bodies of
our soldiers.
Friendly fire? Or military aid to
despotic ex-allies now aiming in our
direction. Arms for Iran. Arms for
Iraq. Violent
cash crop returning to
haunt us.
The nation that prepares for war
finds war.
Prepare for peace.

Some who survive desert hurricane
bring death back home in diseased
platelets. Battalions of
white corpuscles
can't defeat vaccination cocktails
and depleted uranium.
Don't drink the hot chemical
soup formerly known as
diet coke.
Iraq has come back
to the gene bank. Mother's
milk is laced with
anthrax. And a Desert

Storm veteran named McVeigh
once learned
that all's fair in love
and collateral damage. Remember
when bombs lit Oklahoma
City like 4th of July over
no-fly zones?

What will it be, America? Scent of cinnamon
and sandalwood? Or stench of
sulfur and seared
flesh? In Washington DC
Desert Storm sniper
finds bus drivers and suburban
moms in Cold Blue
gunsight. In Fort Bragg, Carolina,
Delta Force family values
decree death for wives
of suicidal killing machines. Boys
don't cry. They just
squeeze
triggers of military madness.
Staccato drumroll of
death. Those who prepare for war
will find war. Prepare
for peace!

All over America, veterans live
in trees and in refrigerator
boxes. Holding signs, "have pneumonia . . .
will work for medicine". 10,000 dead
of desert illness. Populating
prisons and poorhouses.
Princes and queens of Africa.
Royal bloodline of Aztec nations. Noble sons and

daughters of dustbowl
farms. Of mines. Of factories. Skin
blackened with coal dust
and axle grease.

Meanwhile,
old men with soft white hands
make life and death
decisions from safety of
mansions and ranch houses. Maps of
Newark, Detroit, Chicago, and
Los Angeles are soaked with
vital fluids of
the young. Do not drench the
terrain of Arabia with their
blood.
The nation that prepares
for peace will find peace. Prepare
for peace!

America.
You are a glass house. Your
instruments of battle
are bleeding colors of destruction all
over the globe.
Be the beautiful. Be the strong
and the brave. Lay down
your weapons. Be the land of
the free. Remember?
How you
lifted your lamp beside
the golden door?

PART III

Unfurl
the great, fluttering promise
you once made
on that tall ship of state.
So that we might
sail
your irresistible amber
waves far,

far

into the future.

BIG UGLY WAR

Don't send me
I wanna ignore.
What's happenin' out there?
What big, ugly war?

Send all the poor folk.
They can learn to fight.
Don't send me,
I'm wealthy and white!

Those fools without jobs . . .
go to war or go to jail.
I been to college on my
daddy's coattails.

I got a future as an
entrepreneur,
stockbroker, movie actor,
or Texas governor.

"N' us rich guys cain't go.
We're favored 'n' thin.
Your felony life sentence is our
youthful indiscretion.

If it's grim, if it's gruesome,
if it's World War III,
gonna sell some corporate weapons—
make some BIG money. Yes!

PART III

I'm a general in this profitable war,
'n' it really, really suits me, cause
I can catch it in comfort
on TV.

Just ... don't send me!

THE FOLLOWING SEVEN POEMS ARE REPRINTED FROM
"ON THE LIFE OF LINDA J. ALBERTANO:
FROM TRAUMA TO HIGH ART".

BELOVED

Thou art incendiary.
Thou sendest me up in sparks
                100 times a day.
Thou makest me hum like 1000
       buzzing phone lines yammering through
              dizzy night.

When thou smilest upon me, I'm
       money in the bank.
When thou snarlest, I am as a bad
       check, bounced, and cowering
       in thy heart's darkest dumpster.

Thou art the Lion of La Cienega,
       the Rose of Sherman Way.
       I love to lay eyes on thee.

Thou ringest through me sudden
       and bright as fresh champagne.
My switchboard overloadeth.

Thy breath is as clean laundry
       folded behind thy lips.
Thy teeth art as white Cadillacs
       parked in neat rows.

I love to taste the texture
       of thy skin.
Thine eyes art interstellar.

Beloved,
       thou art incendiary.

Thou sendest me up in sparks!

BUSY

(Note to the Reader. Poem to be read in an increasingly rapid word speed.)

"I'm sooo busy," she said.
"I've really been terribly, terribly busy."

"You ha-ave?" remarked her friend,
"Why, what a coincidence,
I've been busy, too. I've been very busy.
Why I've been extremely, extraordinarily busy."

"You've been busy," said a third party,
who was simply eavesdropping on the street.
"You think you've been busy, let me
tell you what busy is. I'm busy.
I am a very busy person.
I have been sooo busy. Why, this year,
I have been busier than I have been
all other years put together.
Just in the first few months, barely.
You can't imagine how frightening it is,
not to be able to have time
to get down to the Discount
App Store. I mean, that's how
very busy I've been!"
"Oh, yeah?" said her friend, "Well,
I have been too busy to have my
smart phone respond to your insulting tweets."

"Oh, yeah?" retorted the very first to speak,

"Well, let me tell you this—I have been too
busy—even to take lunch. I get my meals through
an intravenous hook-up. Next to my desk. Where I work.
At TikTok."

"Oh, yeah? Meanwhile, I been doing
a hundred-and-twenty miles an hour
on the Poetry Superhighway.
Catch me if you can, Copper!"

"Oh, yeah?"

"Oh, yeah?? Well let me tell you
how busy <u>I've</u> been. I have been
frighteningly, astoundingly, shockingly
busy with my very busy
frightening, shocking, and astounding schedule!
There isn't one tiny piece of light
that can shine through any crack
in my schedule. Because I am just . . . I've, I've g . . .
I'm quintuple-booked is how busy <u>I</u> am.
That's how very, very busy I am."

"Because I'm, I'm such busy person,

I've just been really, really busy.
I've been, I've been busier than you can imagine."

"No one <u>knows</u> how busy I've been.
I've been busier than the speed of light.
I've been really, really busy."

"I mean I'm busy. I, I'm so busy.
I'm, I'm . . . Wait! . . . I don't know, I dunno how to,
how to explain how busy I am . . .

I'm really, really busy, I'm very busy.
It's . . . wait, no, HELP! No, WAIT! I'm
too busy, I'm too busy. I've been very busy.
I'm a very busy, busy person! Busy, busy, busy!
don't you understand? I mean <u>busy</u> when I say busy!
I'm not kidding, I'm serious. I mean busy! Really
busy, busy, busy!"

"Wait! Oh, Stop! Oh, Help!
Somebody help me. Somebody.
Somebody stop me. Stop me.
Someone stop me before I <u>do</u>
one more thing!"

GOOD AMERICANS

Good Americans are kind to dogs and children.
Good Americans give to the thoroughly needy.
Good Americans are massively patriotic.
Fine Americans express such tender sympathies.

Good Americans have never harmed a living creature.
Good Americans lead basically blameless lives.
Good Americans are proud of their personal karmas.
Upstanding Americans never hear the screams.

Good Americans tend to their own little gardens.
Good Americans don't count their pit bulls
    before they've hatched
Good Americans breed BMW's for pleasure.
Responsible Americans never drive home through Watts.

Good Americans know that nothing is sacred but style.
Good Americans shop on eBay or Amazon or Saks.
Good Americans own smart phones and second amendment attack drones.
But Loyal Americans own no lampshades of human flesh.

Good Americans are aggressively apathetic.
Good Americans can't hear the children scream.
Good Americans make a business of keeping
    their hands clean.
God-fearing Americans are only doing their jobs.

Good Americans are not their brother's keepers.
Good Americans wear blindfolds on their blindfolds.
Good Americans have front row seats in Heaven.
Decent Americans don't hear the tortured screams.

PART III

Good Americans ask only that god grant them
    the serenity to accept the things
        they cannot change
    and the ability to ignore the things
        they can.

Good Americans

SHE LIKED HER COFFEE . . .

the way she liked her men.

Obsequious and fawning.

I'm parched!

Could you bring me a Dr. Brown's Celery Tonic, please?
(you bring soda bottle on tray).

One that caters to my every whim?
Showers me with emeralds and ermine?
(I take bottle).

Um. Nice head on that tonic.
Ooooops, looks like a hair . . .
(I pull white fur from bottle),

Oh. The fur-lined soda.
(I hand it back).

Thank you, Gordon.
(I wave you away).

Elisha: "It's pronounced Gor-DON."
(and you leave).

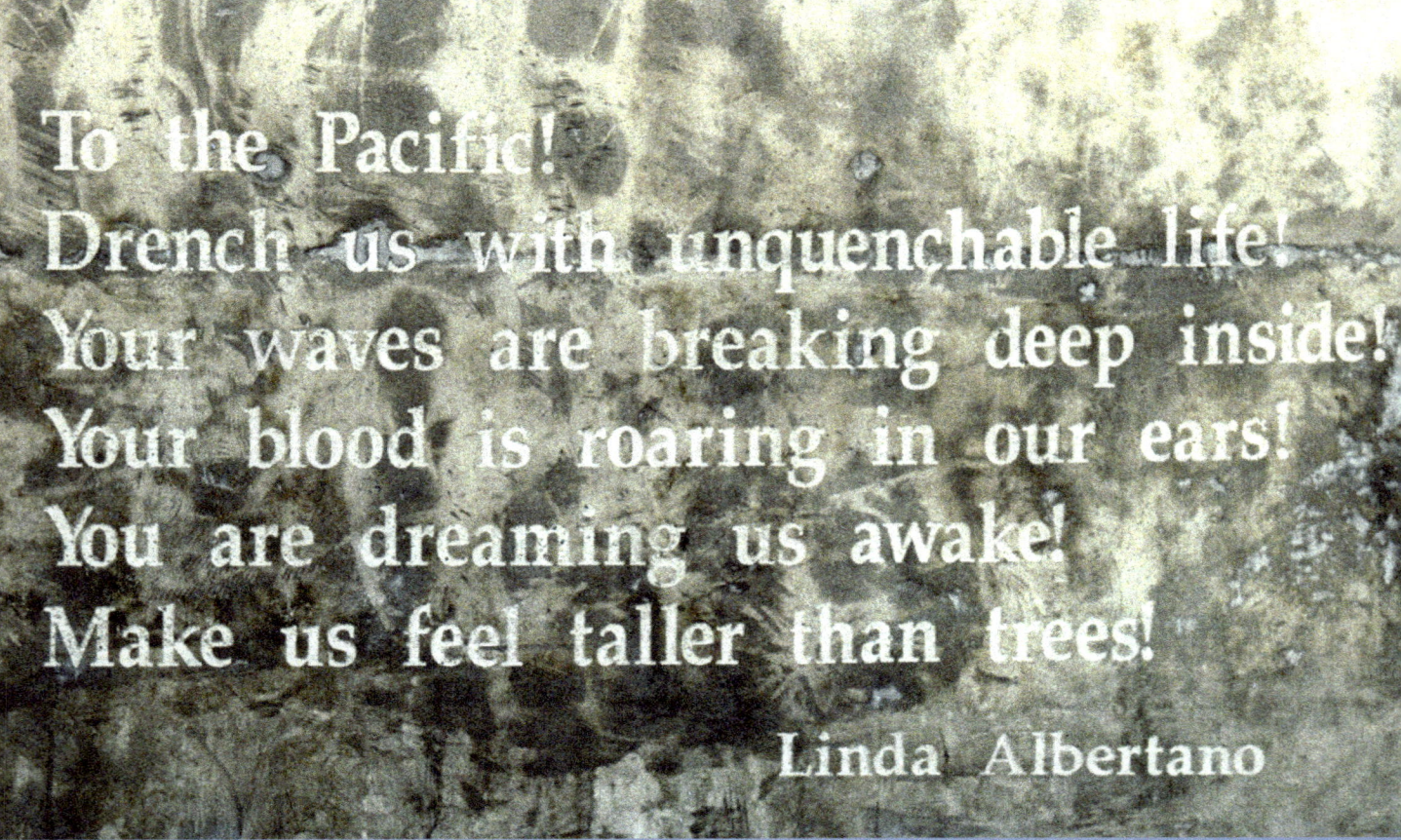

To the Pacific!
Drench us with unquenchable life!
Your waves are breaking deep inside!
Your blood is roaring in our ears!
You are dreaming us awake!
Make us feel taller than trees!

Linda Albertano

Above: Venice Poets' Wall Monument

PART III

TO THE PACIFIC

To the Pacific!
Who is older than wisdom.
Who is shrinking like the slow death of thought.
Who is caught in a storm behind our ribs.
Who finds her rhythm in the delirious
      heartbeat of night.

It's dark.
Where were we when the lights went out?

IT ALL BEGAN WITH CHERRY SOUP

Who poured the last round?
It's dark.
It gets dark in here fast.
 To the Pacific!
Who throbs in our improbable bodies.
Who breathes us in and out.
Who sings between Earth and Orion.
Who makes us feel taller than trees.
Who suffers the weight of our pain.
Who's been trained to submit to our whims.
Whom we'd bring to her knees if she had them.
Who's been trapped in a terminal brothel.
Whom we've cast in an X-rated movie
       and we're waiting to watch her bleed.

It's dark.
By the nature of our deeds we're dirty.
We're bound in our own senseless chains.
It's dark. How long can this last?
It's sad. Is it criminal? Or criminally insane?
It's dark in here.
It gets dark in here fast.

To the Pacific!
Who surprised us with the curious
invention of life.
Whose intentions were purely honorable.
Who stirred our first shimmering cells.
Who helped us crawl up on her shores.
Whose blood still roars in our ears.
Whom we've caged like a laboratory rabbit   blinded with stinging rain.
We're boys pulling wings from sparrows
       obliviously nonchalant.
We spend her like sailors on benders
       ignoring her desperate eyes.

She's kidnapped for the intangible joyride.
She's dropped in the vestigial ditch.
How quickly we tire of our toys.

It gets dark.
It gets dark in here fast.
We are pushing her past her prime.
We shout petrochemical lies!
Time sticks in our indecent throats.
It gets dark, it gets dark, it gets dark in here fast.
And where were we when the lights went out?
Where were we?

To the Pacific . . .
      to her we belong!

She holds no wrongheaded notion of justice.
She builds no concrete tomb for our lungs.
She forces us to feed on no poison.
She hangs us from no twisted tree.
She rids us of no personal medfly.
She plants no bomb in our gut.
She crushes no skull for freedom.
She nails us not to the ground.
She studies us not into extinction.
Her changes are slower than rivers.
History melts in her mouth.
She'd deliver us from evil if we'd let her.
How long have we been lost?
And where were we when the lights went out?

It's dark. It's dark.
It gets dark in here fast.

To the Pacific!

You are bluer than our insignificant eyes.
You are saltier than the tears we cried
      when we heard you might die of
our neglect.
We're killing you with exquisite indifference.
You've washed our feet with your grief.
We're gathered on the courthouse steps.
We're bargaining one more plea.
We're praying they'll spare you from us.
Our blood is screaming your name!
We're tearing up the deed to your being.
We'll love you more deeply than death.
We're prepared to pay the better price.
We'll rip the tainted needles from our veins.
Our blood is screaming, is screaming your name!

We are about to become more serious.
Where were we when the lights went out?

To the Pacific!
Older than unbearable wisdom.
Shrinking like the pointless death of thought.
Caught in the fire storm in our heads.
Tattooing the sacred skin of night.
Pounding in our hopeful bodies.
Breathing us in and out.
Shouting Hosannas under Orion!

Drench us with unquenchable life!
Your waves are breaking deep inside!
Your blood is roaring in our ears!
You are dreaming us awake!
Make us feel taller than trees!
Dance us in your pagan arms!
Your drums are beating on our shores!

We're comprehending what you'd have us do!
We're sounding louder alarms!
We long to be truer believers!
We'll be strong in our will to prevail!
And we belong, we belong, we belong to you!
It's to you that we belong!

You've made your mark on our souls.

But it's dark in here.
Don't let the lights go out.
We're about to become more serious.
Don't let the light disappear.

Don't ever
let the light

disappear.

VALENTINE'S DAY WITH LUCIFER

Valentine's Day
but there will be no sweetheart
bouquets for the lady.
There will be no lacy white doilies, no
chocolate creams in a blood
red box. Cupid
will be hung upside
down from the attic
rafters.

Lucifer throws the dice. He
bets when <u>this</u> day
is done you'll be broken
into bits.
Lucifer wins. Lucifer
always wins.

Unholy thoughts twist
in him like luminous
corkscrews.

He
is the serial
killer of your every innocent
moment. He
murders you as he
would a sleeping
schoolgirl. He
is a cannibal tasting
joy when he sucks on your l
cerebellum. Your
grief is his midnight
snack. Watching the life

PART III

slip away from
your life sends champagne
through his fluted
capillaries. Oh Charm! He
is serpent
as movie star. Jake
LaMotta as purveyor
of the big lie. He
will set you up for
the sucker
punch with another, "Baby,
I love you." You
will die straightjacketed
with pain as in Houdini's
last trick. And you
will believe him
everytime. You
have swallowed more sewage
than the law allows. Do
not drink from your
own contaminated waters. Fish
float belly up on your bloated
shores.

And still . . .
      you're back for more?

You
have chosen a black
wedding
over an exorcism.
Now your mistake has you
staked to the ground. Jackals
gnaw on your entrails
for entertainment.

Valentine's Day,
but Lucifer allows no
couplets exchanged, no
pastel candy hearts marked
with a pink "be mine," no
florid cards in frilly
envelopes.

For this occasion fifty
roses will be blackened
in the blast furnace within his
chest. You
will be hog-tied for a demented
cross-examination. You
will be boiled in the false
crucible of his
suspicion.

Outside pedestrians shudder at
the torment of your
cries. He
will be unmoved by *your*
tenderness or your
terror.
When it's over you'll
be discarded with yesterday's
news. And
later
you'll remember his
hair
smoking through your breathless
fingers and
you'll know a strange
agony
of emptiness.

Should the shy boys
come to collect
their kisses, you'll turn
them away and push your
face into a wet
pillow
to crush your noisy
loneliness. You'll miss
the taste of
sulfur and his brimstone
breath riding across your
shoulders through the red
eye of night. You won't
know
if your bones are burning
down to ash from the heat of your
love or of your
hatred.

Deep
in the mineshaft of his demonic
universe Lucifer
hums a tune. He
is wearing white and
preparing a meal for two. His
next victim, resplendently
brunette, is
recumbent on velveteen
cushions. He'll seduce her with
white fish and dark
language, basil and lime
juice, juniper berries and black love
incense. Jake
LaMotta as serpent. He

sets her up for the knockout, "Baby,
Baby, I love you."

She
slides into his
snare. She thinks of bassinets and
of growing old
together. He thinks of trussing
her tightly and of slow-roasting
her on a spit for
the holidays. She tumbles
into his trap. He
can't wait to hear her simple
screams. He
looks forward to
Thanksgiving. He
has much reason to be thankful. Lucifer
wins. No need to toss
the dice this time. Lucifer
wins again—Lucifer <u>always</u>
wins.

Valentine's Day.
Lucifer says he loves you.
But there will be no
bouquet
for the lady.

VIRTUE

Virtue rides into town on a
convertible Clydesdale. She's wrapped
in blue-and-white
stars
and is eating an apple concoction.
Ah, Virtue! They want
you.
Your symbols
are so succulent! They want to use
you
for purposes of personal
adornment. They want to pin
you,
wholesome and lovely, to their lapels.

Virtue drinks nothing but
water
from glaciers and the sap of lacebark
pine.
Ah, Virtue. You're deep
in danger. Of becoming a dull
boy.
Everyone knows
the most fascinating females are
hookers
with hearts of gold. They smoke
their cheroots and sing in their
whiskey
tenors. They wear flamingo
lipstick
and kiss your boyfriend on the mouth.

Virtue goes to a square
dance
with the cleanest of all the
cowboys.
Outside, dark-eyed men
lurk
smelling of rum
and rosewater. Ah, Virtue!
Don't let them handle
you
with their hot hands!

Virtue wears a starched
blouse
and a pristine pair of gloves to
church. A silver
cross
in the crook of her neck. Virtue is
dainty.
She kneels at the altar. She swallows the
blood
and the body of Christ. Ah,
Virtue!

At the far end of the road,
they've masked a
sinner
and paraded him as you. You! Who
are as creamy and innocent as
milk.
Don't let them
leave you too long in the
sun!

Don't let them hang any
heretics
in your name!

Virtue has blue, blue eyes. And genuine
blonde hair. She's the
Virgin
Spring. Really. Is that fair?
I mean. She never wears gardenia
perfume.
She doesn't know how to swing
a hammer. But she looks
delectable
on the couch in any living room. I
worry
about you, Virtue. Are you tasting the
juice of life? Are you afraid to
stain
the bib of your dress?

Oh, Virtue. Run! Run before
they snare you in their pious and
hellish
nets! Save yourself, Virtue! They want to use
you for purposes of
narcissism.
They want to turn you upside-down
and imprison you in their green and glorious
gore.
Their hounds are howling
in the hills! Hide! Be the
purloined
letter, Virtue. They can't hurt you
if they can't see you. They can't see you if you're everywhere.

IT ALL BEGAN WITH CHERRY SOUP

Be everywhere, Virtue.
Be nowhere.   Be something.   Be nothing.   Hide.
Ride
out of town on a white Clydesdale.   Ah,
Virtue.   We love your girlish
ways!

Don't ever change.

PART IV
STORIES BY LINDA J. ALBERTANO

THE QUEEN OF TEETH

Dear Charles,

On the road with Alice Cooper. I be real evil six nights a week. The crowd loves the badness to pieces. 20,000 strong, times three nights in a row, at Joe Lewis Stadium in Detroit. From behind the Sludge Monster's cage, I see 1,000 points of light. Not the Presidential speech kind. No. More like the rebellious rock-fan roach lighter kind.

As the cruel Nurse Ratchet, I shove a doll-baby in its carriage onto the stage. Soon the doll will be impaled at the end of a sword for the winsome tune, "Dead Babies." But for now, I pluck its formula from its tiny mitts and brandish the bottle fiendishly above my head. Except for the night they secretly substitute a dildo for the baby bottle, and I find myself waving a wobbly large-caliber rubber thing at the cheering crowd.

Later, when Alice is trussed in a straitjacket, I'll stomp up behind him armed with a giant syringe. Kicking him to his knees, I'll plunge the trick needle deep into his neck and draw out what appears to be a gallon of blood. I'm despicable! The audience is delirious with hatred.

Then, as I scratch furious notes on a clipboard, Alice slips from his bindings and throws them around my neck. I flail! I gasp! I tug at the garrote at my throat! I claw at the air with both hands! Finally, I collapse. A colossal roar of approval erupts from 20,000 tattooed, pierced, and slavering fans! And so I am dragged away, a glow of perfect achievement inwardly warming me.

After the show, a devotee will invite Alice to a party. "Thanks," he'll respond, "but I've got an embalming to get to."

Dee-troit! We crash in the Omni Hotel. Oh, Detroit. Detroit. Where covered catwalks high above the city lead to luxury eateries and displays of opulence heretofore unimagined. But. In Detroit. If you push open a door at ground level, you'll enter a world of squalor and despair populated by hobos and costermongers, cut-purses and down-n-outers. Where the clerk at the corner convenience store cowers behind double layers of bulletproof glass.

We live in relative splendor on the tour bus . . . furnished with refrigerator, indoor plumbing, tables and captain's chairs, TVs and DVD players PLUS two ultra-comfy lounges separated by cozy, stacked bunkbeds where we sleep after each show while the bus whistles through the dark to our next gig. We do six cities a week—a clock whose second hand is rapidly spinning. When we learn that Luther Vandross stays one full week at each stop—a clock ticking verrry slowly—we're incredulous and envious.

But on we roll, to Phoenix, where leaves rustling across the sidewalk whisper, "Barry Goldwater, Barry Goldwater." Of course, today, they'd whisper "Joe Arpaio, Joe Arpaio." But that was then, and people still remembered.

We get a one-day holiday in Breaux Bridge, Louisiana. I drop in to Mulate's for red beans and rice only to discover Dewey Balfa and Brothers singing their lids off in Cajun French and every living body, adolescent or ancient, small or tall, frail or burly is whooping it up, dancing as though one foot is nailed to the floor while the other gyrates wildly! "Chank-a-Chank!" as they say in zydeco.

In Cleveland, where department store clerks actually assist you, I fell in love with a white-haired gentleman in the luggage aisle. I'd have married him on the spot, but he wouldn't sign a prenup, and that was a deal-breaker.

I jest. Performers are the lettuce-pickers of the entertainment industry. So the dancer, the sludge-monsters and the evil nurse earn just enough to keep them in heavy metal jewelry and black eye shadow. Shopping is what you do on the road in a new town in the afternoon before the show. Alice Cooper knows the location of every "Chess King" extreme accouterment retail store in America!

Rolling across farmland, we see the names of porno-flicks hand-painted on the side of a barn in thick, crooked black letters. Instead of roadside produce in the bucolic landscape, we're offered bushels of flesh. Alice slides open a window and shouts, "What's this, America? We give you the Farm Aid Concert and you give us, 'Debbie does Dallas'!?"

So when we get to Chicago, I decide to explore a local porn shop. I look tough in a long, khaki army overcoat, working the stub of a frayed cigar into lip cancer. I shoulder my way to the back where the magazine rack stands. A ragged line of guys are fingering the plastic covers with their hot hands. Yeah.

At six-foot-four-inches tall, I tower over all of them. I'm like the monolith in the *Space Odyssey* movie. I catch a few startled glances whilst I paw through the goods. I see porn of every description from tasteful Rubenesque erotica to grainy black and white newsprint pix of the private parts of 80-year-old grannies. Something for everyone! I purchase a couple of handsome gay-guy mags for me and the whip-dancer and take my leave.

All the performers and band members on the bus are into health and fitness. Alice put down Johnny Walker for good after he was found living in a motel wearing a diaper and sporting six-inch fingernails. Now he imbibes only juice and soft drinks that he, himself has opened for fear of unknown and pernicious spiking of his beverages. The lead guitarist, Kane Roberts, is a genuine big-biceped bodybuilder. Kip Winger, the bass player, is as beautiful as a matinee idol and intends to keep it that way. So, conversation on the band bus goes like, "Hey. Where'd you score the low-fat cottage cheese?"

The crew, however, still bears the torch of decadence aloft. They're men who've skirmished with luck and lost. Their bodies sag like spent mattresses. Their smiles are full of black holes, dense and massive. No illicit substance, no general debasement, no off-limits act is too depraved for their amusement.

We've been touring with White Snake, Guns and Roses, Alien Sex Fiend, and assorted bands with Big Hair. One of whom brings a naked groupie decorated with whipped cream into the dressing room on a dessert trolley. As the tour feminist, I feel compelled to pull her aside afterwards and encourage her to form a union with the other groupies. After all. They ought to be remunerated for their labors.

And because the destination on the front of the bus reads "Show Us Your Tits" (all in fun, of course, but it engages me). So, Sylvia, the lovely whip-dancer and I make bumper-stickers for the back of the bus reading, "Reveal Testes or Perish."

When I appear in my bald-headed wig as the black-robed executioner, I am Regina Dentata, the Queen of Teeth! Soon Alice Cooper will be dragged to my guillotine and strapped down there while I raise the blade. Then, whoosh! As if by magic his cranium will roll into the basket at my feet. I'll snatch it by the hair, and make a dramatic show of kissing his dripping, gory lips. I'll stride to the edge of the stage holding his head high and grinning diabolically. Then, I'll reach into his cold, dead skull to squeeze a bulb filled with a viscous red fluid which Alice's grim head will vomit into the screaming, writhing crowd. The End.

Except that Alice is resurrected in white tails and a top hat for the anthem, "School's Out for Summer." His disciples are ecstatic! The stone has been rolled away from the mouth of the cave, and the cave is empty . . . Easter has come early this year. Good times!

I keep having this dream. For a prank, I take Alice's fake head to a party. The door is thrown open, but no one laughs. They're horrified. I look down and realize . . . I have the wrong head. It's someone else's real dismembered head.

Hey! Long Beach in three weeks. Hope you can make it. Wear a blood-bib anywhere in the first three rows. And be sure to stay for the embalming after the show . . .

Hugs,

Linda J.
Evil Nurse and Executioner

FLYING INTO GUINEA

I had played rhythm kora behind Prince Diabate for a time when he longed to hear the fat, round tones of the bolon, the West African contrabass in his band. So he asked me to join him on a trip to Africa to study with Amadou Bolon, the greatest living traditional West African bass player on the planet.

Dust. Dust and more dust. We flew into Guinea during the dry and dusty season. From the air West Africa was a dusty, sepia-toned photograph. Dust and the color of dust. Dust covered every branch, leaf, vine, and growing thing. Dust on every inanimate object. A film of dust covered the Mangrove trees, their tangled roots looming larger and larger as we lowered into the airport.

Which was a scene of havoc and humanity with a crush of beings claiming luggage, hand over head, in a cacophony of languages. French, Malinke, Puehl, Fulani, Baga, Wolof, and Susu. I was bewildered. But Prince Diabate was there to greet us with someone to manage the bags and a host of high-spirited singers, drummers, and dancers. This was not your typical scene at LAX.

We piled into a waiting car to drive into the city. On both sides of the road were people walking. They walk distances in Africa. In the open fields, women strode in the dust, bearing pallets of eggs and oranges, babies and baskets slung across their backs. One man carried his entire store of maps and books on his head and body in a specially designed multi-pocketed mufti.

It was dusk . . . the traditional time of cleaning the streets and byways. Bundles of twigs were used to sweep the day's trash into countless heaps. Which were then cremated. Pewter smoke curled into a deepening pewter sky like the prayers of pilgrims rising from the banks of the River Styx. To my eyes, it was astonishing and marvelous.

Soon, roadside shops sprouted and grew thicker until suddenly, we were in the capital city, Conakry, which was home to a million souls. However, due to the sporadic nature of the electrical supply, there were no signal lights in the streets. I have often seen brave policemen stare down onrushing traffic in an unflinching game of chicken. And win!

When we arrived near the center of Conakry, we pulled off the road into . . . what? On one side . . . a painted concrete building shared a wide dirt lot with clotheslines filled with cheerful prints. On the other, a six-foot iron gate. Which slid open and voila! We were home!

The Motel du Port was ingeniously constructed of cargo containers with doors and windows cut through and a wall dividing them into duplex units. I was to live in relative splendor with one of the few air conditioners in the city and a trickle of heated water in the shower.

Prince Diabate is worshipped in West Africa. He's treated like a combination of Elvis and the Pope. He had to change living quarters every day or two to keep his fans at bay while he slept.

But every day, Amadou Bolon arrived at the Motel du Port for my lesson. Since I spoke no Malinke, Puehl, Fulani, Baga, Wolof or Susu, and he spoke no English, I learned by watching his hands. Then, when I understood some part of the pattern, I practiced and practiced to coax my hands into mimicking his.

The first song he showed me was Sankouman which looked like a combination of boxing and chopping.

SANKOUMAN
I finally got that it was choreography. Playing the bolon was a dance of the hands. This was driven home when he taught me his solo which he played on one string, and which I will faithfully reproduce for you here.

SOLO
Next, I learned

SABOU
And FASO

And here's a damping technique in BARAKI

Most kora concerts are sedate with the kora master seated on stage
playing gorgeous celestial sounds
for an hour. But Prince Diabate is far more dynamic.
Young and energetic, he's known as the Jimi Hendrix
of the kora.

When we played the Getty, fans stood up, knocked their chair seats back and danced in place until the joint was throbbing. The curator was flabbergasted. It was the first and only time THAT had ever happened.

In 2010, just before he moved to France, we played our last show at Grand Performances in the California Plaza. So he was in Europe for four years until this July when he returned for an intimate evening at Motherland Music, LA's marketplace and mecca for West African drums and dancing.
It's a small place which, including standing room, held only 60 people.

At first, the audience was subdued, bobbing their heads in time with the music. Then a brave soul or two would venture a turn around the dance floor. Finally random drummers leapt from their seats and began to pound on Motherland's array of instruments until the building began to shake.

The rhythm GUITAR was going chucka-chucka, chucka-chucka, chuckety-chuck, chucka-chucka . . .

and the BALAFON went . . .

and the BASS DRUMS went . . .

and the DJEMBE went tuk tukka thwack, tuk tukka thwack, tukka tukka tukka thwack . . .

and the TALKING DRUM went going, gagoing-going . . .

Meanwhile, Prince's fingers were exploding on the strings. Everyone was dancing and dollar bills were raining down on the stage (which is how griots get paid).

HERAKOURA

So, DANCE, my friend. You're in West Africa. DANCE.

Griots were the official kora players and the King's Counsel. They're the oral historians and the living encyclopedias of West Africa. They say that when a griot dies, it's as though a library has burned down.

MY SAFARI (GUINEA, WEST AFRICA)

I'm staying at the Motel du Port near downtown Conakry, the capital of Guinea, West Africa. I'm in a duplex unit. That is, my room has been made from one-half of a metal shipping container, fitted with a door, windows, and a modest bathroom. The walls are shiny with dark, faux-mahogany shelf paper, edges curling with heat and age. A single bulb struggles to illuminate the center of the room, at least during those times when the electricity is operational.

My host, Prince Diabate, has billeted me in one of only two units in the entire complex with air conditioning and a trickle of hot water in the shower. When there is water. But I'm fortunate to live here in relative splendor, for I've seen grand mansions in Conakry with fewer amenities. Gated homes with chandeliers hung from high ceilings. With great stone lions frozen in front, eyeing gazelles lounging on the grounds forever out of reach. I'm happy here at the Motel du Port where I have everything I want, including a fuzzy throw rug by my bed to step on when I wake.

At night, I crawl beneath mosquito netting and tuck its edges under the mattress from inside. There, under a gauzy white canopy, I'm safe, for the moment, from malaria-bearing insects. Oh, I've sprayed with malathion on a weekly basis. And morning will reward me with the bodies of one or two kamikaze mosquitoes hanging needle nose-first in the net. They've been inexorably drawn to their deaths by the seductive scent of carbon dioxide exhaled as I lay sleeping. With unholy satisfaction, I imagine little "x"s on their tiny eyes as I flick them into oblivion before undertaking my ablutions.

The net also protects me from small mammals that skitter across linoleum in the dark. The mice have eaten my hard boiled eggs, my protein supplement, and my vitamin C. They are now more perfectly nourished than any human who dwells in the capital city. I can only assume that, over time, they're developing a collective immune system, mighty as King Kong's. Ordinarily, I like mice, and I'm happy to share my provisions with them. But they've taken to eating the antelope parts of my rare, one-of-a-kind, handmade musical instrument, the West African contrabass (known as the bolon), and this is an activity that unalterably alienates me.

I take the advice of the motel manager, Monsieur Soumah, who looks like an African Tom Wolfe, tall and intelligent, in his white suit. He tells me to set out packets of poisoned peanuts nightly. Unfortunately, this serves only to increase the numbers of the mouse tribe, and their skittering now resembles a victory march, multiple talons of an invincible horde, across the floor. Listening to the rumble of claws under my bed after midnight, I realize that the vitamins and amino acids have simply enabled them to withstand the assault of any amount of poisoned pellets on their diminutive, yet powerful, digestive tracts. I assume word has gone out to the entire rodent kingdom that there is an ongoing feast in unit 10. No doubt the drumming of their skinny tails on the plumbing is a kind of telegraphy rivaling Western Union. Ultimately, they win. I'm forced to hang the bolon from the ceiling, where only mice with suction cups on the palms of their paws will have access.to it. Fortunately, I will have taken the instrument back to America before evolution grants them the ability to devour all its edible parts.

One night, I sit outside playing the music I've so recently learned and watching a couple of motel cats meander in the courtyard. A slim white feline sits about three feet away from me lazily grooming herself. Suddenly from under the shipping container-slash-motel room across the way, a hulking, sinister, gray shape appears and shoots across the yard between the cat and me. I shriek as I see its ugly naked tail disappear under the floor of my bedroom. It's true that I like mice. But I fear rats. This one would've flattened the cat. It was even bigger than rats I'd seen running ceiling pipelines like fat tightrope walkers in restaurant kitchens I'd worked back home.

I flew to the manager and begged for the giant, industrial steel-spring trap I'd once seen in his office. But he spoke French. And since "oui" and "bonjour" and "au revoir" are my primary tools of communication in that language, I was forced to make a large trap shape with my hands. And then snap it shut like the jaws of death to illustrate it's mighty spring-action. But the elegant Monsieur Soumah was unfazed. He tidied his counter and swept an errant paper clip out of sight. Fantasizing that I actually knew the French word for rat, I gibbered "el raton! el raton!" in high school Spanish while flailing my arms in the general direction of its disappearance. But, alas, the trap would not be forthcoming.

Monsieur Soumah placed his fingers together. And in his deepest and most deluxe French accent, said simply, "Welcome to Africa." It was then that I realized ... this was my African Safari. Here in the most urban place in Guinea, far from any lion or tiger or hippopotamus, distant from the trumpeting of any elephant or even from a single rapid-fire monkey declaration, I was experiencing wildlife in an exotic and distant land.

What could possibly be better than this?

WALKABOUT
Linda in West Africa

Every morning before the sun grew insurmountably aggressive, I'd walk through Conakry One, that part of the city which juts into the sea like a large earthen thumb bravely staking its claim in an immensity of water. Three sides of Conakry One have ocean views. On foot, it was possible to traverse the city from northern coastline to southern in a couple of hours. Usually, I'd stick to the main streets—Boulevard de Independence and Rue du Commerce where the commercial buildings actually were to be found—Air France, a couple of banks and jewelry stores, as well as the coffee house and an internet cafe.

I'd wander past decaying, century-old French buildings whose balconies and peeling walls were redolent of New Orleans; past the crumbling train station, abandoned but for a few muscular, rusting engine cars; proud as massive draft horses, still tingling with phantom wheel pain and, within their iron hearts, still singing anthems to the rails. They dream of a nobler past, when Sekou Toure ran the trains on time and thought of nothing else but the well-being and prosperity of his constituents. Now, the trains and the people of Guinea must rely on the good will of Lansana Conte, who, at the moment, is reserving it for himself and a few close friends.

I'd pass intriguing merchant stalls of clothing, leather goods, handwoven mats, kitchenwares, and food; women making fish or chicken stew; women making fonio (which is something like millet) and sauce; oh, the scent of fresh beignets, hot little donuts fried right on the spot; and oranges, on every corner, women peeling just the color off piles of fresh oranges, turning them into white orbs of juicy pleasure that are the foremost fast-food of Guinea. Oranges to be sucked dry and discarded, and oranges whose withered corpses accumulate in the streets until day's end when each entrepreneur stoops to sweep the area clean again with a bundle of straw and twigs gripped in one hand.

And the dress! The fabric! Guinea may be one of the poorest countries in Africa, but many of its denizens appear to have just stepped from a neat new bandbox. Each costume is consummately crafted in designs green and pink, turquoise and blue, mango and purple, indigo, vivid yellow, or red! I'd inhale these musical patterns of wearable art daily as I walked past moneychangers, beggars, and purveyors of mysterious trinkets.

I never saw another Anglo-Saxon or European strolling about the streets. Unless I stepped inside a western-style restaurant or hotel, I'd have no sense that these places were host to Russian, French, Belgian, Canadian, and all manner of businessmen who parked their Lexus or Lincoln SUVs out front, next to wet laundry spread flat on the sidewalks to dry. No one used the sidewalks anyway. Pedestrians shared the streets with teams of soccer-playing kids who dodged around cars or bounced balls right off their windshields. Rolling blackouts have left the city entirely without stoplights. But everyday courageous policemen stand in the center of primary intersections and work to unsnarl a tangle of converging trucks and autos. To maintain order, they plant themselves firmly in the paths of errant drivers in a take-no-prisoners game of chicken in which the cops invariably prevail.

In Guinea, Prince Diabate's fame is akin to that of Elvis. Or the Pope. Or some combination thereof. Whereas America is a place that can swallow a great musician without so much as a burp, from the moment the Air France craft bearing Prince touched down on the tarmac, his countrymen immediately sensed his presence. He lit up their synapses like sunrise on the Savannah. And neither the dreadlocks cultivated in LA, nor the Hollywood shades, nor even the borrowed red beater he tooled around town in could conceal him from the well-honed tracking instincts of his devoted apostles. He did his best to maintain enough privacy to sleep at night by switching lodgings every few days.

As he drove through town, small cadres of admirers often chased behind shouting "Prince, Prince" in accents French and Malinke, SouSou, Fulani, or Baga. Or, whenever his dusty, rolling red relic was at rest, they would congregate nearby. The car itself had become imbued with a princely aura. In fact, once Prince had returned the vehicle, it reappeared with its actual owner, who was often accused of car theft, and has since sworn never to loan it again. At least not to Prince. Who swims innocently in a bubbling current of renown, while devotees, swirling and bobbing in his wake, surface at unexpected moments.

Once, as we feasted on monkfish and haricots verts under an arbor in Les Jardins de Guinea, a trembling acolyte appeared at our table, a supplicant awaiting a Princely blessing. Or a miscreant longing for absolution. Clearly, some kind of torment boiled within him. Prince asked a few questions in their shared tongue. The young man answered briefly. Still appearing to churn internally, he stood for a moment, eyes dark and haunted, before he wheeled and bolted back out through the door from which he'd entered.

Weeks later, at the Motel du Port, I'd face a similarly suffering soul. A refugee from Sierra Leone, the single remaining survivor of her entire family's massacre, clung to me and wept, "I want to go with you to America! Please, please take me there!" And I choked with the competing instincts of wishing to comply and the impossibility of doing so. And in this nation of congenitally happy citizens, I was puzzled by deep sadness in the eyes of one tall and handsome young man. Until I saw the scars across his throat . . . another refugee from Sierra Leone.

Conakry was an even more intense experience for Prince. He was beset by enthusiasts; some seeking merely to touch the hem of his garment, others wanting full hands-on healings. And I, ringed within the halo of his fame, became an instant celebrity.

So, while mine was the only white face on the streets, whenever I took my daily trek, I had dozens of unofficial minders watching my progress and reporting back to Prince. "I saw her near the bank, in the coffeehouse, at the newsstand." His minions, having once glimpsed us together, would now shout "Prince, Prince!" at me as I passed. And near the French Hotel Independence, an assemblage of tour guides yelled their inquiry from across the street.

"Êtes-vous l'étranger de Prince?"

To which I responded, *"Oui. C'est moi. Je suis l'étranger de Prince."*

"Yes. It's me. I'm the foreigner of Prince."

And it filled me with a curious kind of pride to report that "I . . . in fact, am Prince's Stranger."

PART IV

NHA TRANG

We flew, strapped to the floor or to jump seats in stout C-130s, at an altitude of 20,000 feet to avoid incoming anti-aircraft fire. When nose-diving to the edge of a sawed-off mountaintop, there was always that "hold your breath" moment when we first met the nearest rim of the makeshift airstrip. The pilot had to slam his shuddering craft into reverse as soon as his front wheels kissed the peak's granite lip to prevent plunging, snout over teakettle, down an abyss at the other end of the absurdly short strip. Landings and takeoffs were the most perilous as they would bring us well within firing range.

There were seven of us in this particular USO troupe. Shannon and I were folksingers. A drummer, bass player, dancer, comic, and MC completed our raggedy band of entertainers. We were sent to select bases in East and Southeast Asia . . . Japan, Korea, the Philippines, Thailand, and Vietnam. Where children were the barometers of the cultural weather and attitude of each country.

In Japan, we were politely ignored. In the Philippines, I was startled to find school kids filing out of their homes behind me as I strolled a dirt road in the evening. Even more surprising was their spontaneous singing . . . "do, a deer, a female deer; re, a drop of golden sun . . . " voices riding starward in the balmy air as we walked. And in Korea, youngsters gleefully mobbed us, giggling and grinning, whenever we appeared on the street.

But in Vietnam, where you'd be as exposed in an open-faced cyclo as an oyster on the half-shell, small gangs of wrathful children would descend upon you shouting, "Give me money!" And you'd part with the black market piasters you'd so recently bargained for in a somber shop on the Street of Flowers behind the Majestic Hotel in Saigon.

Soldiers who'd been assigned to escort us, however, were of a more homogeneous temperament no matter where we landed. Our chaperones were not the narrow-shouldered boys glimpsed at the back of a mess hall perusing a frayed copy of *Siddhartha*. No. Our hosts were louder and prouder. And now they'd been launched scattershot into distant lands where everyone was a "foreigner."

In the center of Seoul, our jeep driver burst from the army compound gunning his motor through a congested intersection, laughing as terrified pedestrians fled in every direction. In Vietnam, I turned away from the pornography of documented "kills." But I couldn't avoid seeing chicken wire and barbs from behind which local faces peered. We were admonished not to be too curious. "Don't ask," was already a watchword.

It was easy to feel clumsy and coarse around the diminutive Vietnamese. Their streets were filled with willowy manual laborers. We saw no trucks moving to and from construction sites. Instead, slim women in graceful dresses over pajama pants were the preferred methods of conveyance. Waterfalls of black hair cascaded from under their flattened conical hats, and they each carried a pole over one shoulder. From the ends of which hung small pallets of bricks as balanced as scales in the hands of Justice.

Mostly we flew once or twice a day in muscular cargo planes, the C-130 workhorses. Occasionally we were helicoptered to an outlying camp. Or we'd travel by jeep down a jungle road passing clusters of South Vietnamese soldiers, so slight in their uniforms, they looked like Boy Scouts earning their wilderness badges. We were issued M-16 rifles in the event we'd need to defend ourselves against a Viet-Cong ambush.

"Never roll into a ditch at the side of the road," cautioned the soldier behind the wheel. "Or you'll be impaled on fire-hardened bamboo stakes planted there." But we were untrained in the use of weaponry, so the rifles were simply props on our laps as one USO troupe fatally learned the following year on the very same road.

On our travels, we sang in theaters filled with hundreds of servicemen. We also sang in tents, and in hospitals and in mess halls. We even sang from the back of a flatbed truck in the middle of the jungle where an audience of soldiers in combat gear and helmets, rifles over their shoulders stood in a semicircle around us. Until an order was quietly given mid-song, and they melted into the dark and dappled green of the primordial forest.

We were up early and often chewing our way through the air to Da Nang, Khe Sanh, Bien Hoa, Pleiku, Ton Son Nhut and destinations too small and too numerous to be named. We were also given breaks, staying for an extra day here and there to relax. The most memorable of which was Nha Trang, a rest and recreation area for armies of both the North and South.

Nha Trang! Where red and golden sunsets bled like crazy into the bay, lighting the sails of Chinese Junks from behind as they floated there.

Nha Trang! Where clean and glittering waters, generous beaches, lazy palms, and easy weather gave rise to a Bali Hai of relentless beauty.

Nha Trang! Where public walkways were lined with fruit-bearing trees from which I pulled a purple mangosteen or two marveling at its fleshy texture and tart-sweet taste. I dropped in to a local shop to sample some banana-flavored water buffalo yogurt and to buy a pack of sour umeboshi plum gum.

The soldier to whom I'd been assigned was Sergeant Battle. I could scarcely believe the irony. But he invited me to dine with him and a few Vietnamese army officers that evening, and I was delighted at the prospect!

That afternoon I donned a swimsuit to wade into the transparent sea in front of the hotel. Once I was rib-deep, a gaggle of children began mercilessly splashing me. I volleyed back, and we all laughed and carried on. Then two of them separated from their crew and joined up on my side of the imaginary line. Now it was a fair and furious fight! Exhausted after a time, we all crawled out of the water and went our ways. My two comrades-in-arms walked with me to my door. Holding thumbs up, they declared, "You numbah one cô bé!" meaning "girl." With pleasure I shook their small hands before entering the hotel.

After changing, I decided to promenade the byways once more. And there they were! Agleam in fresh shirts and pants and wearing glad smiles. We window-shopped through the modest downtown, happy as three musketeers. At a tailor shop, they chose fabric they liked and were measured for new shirts. The proprietor promised they could retrieve their gifts once he'd finished them. On we went until we came to an ice cream stand. Oboy! While we waited for our cones, Minh tapped both his and his sister's chests. Gesturing toward me, he made a great swooping arc with his arm like a plane flying across the ocean.

"Numbah one!" he exclaimed again.

To be sure, Nha Trang itself was a paradise. But who wouldn't want to flee the rest of that pock-marked, bombed-out, agent-oranged, barbed-wired land? I wanted to smuggle them away in my duffle bag. Still, you don't get to find children on the street like a pair of hungry kittens and take them home with you.

Now I was heading back. I left Quyan and Minh licking their cones and hurried to meet the Sergeant.

The café, though small, could've come straight from the set of *Casablanca*. A ceiling fan twirled above and a friendly gecko parked on the whitewashed wall beside us. Our lobster dinners would be two dollars each. I was charmed by the refined and literate officers as they recited delicate poems and sang traditional songs in English and Vietnamese in their lovely, lilting voices. I couldn't imagine our troops doing the same at a local restaurant unless well-primed with libations. And in two languages? Not likely. Chaos would most certainly ensue.

As dinner came to an end, I thanked my hosts and Sergeant Battle for a singular evening, and we walked the one block back to the hotel. My two pals were once again waiting by the door, radiant in the moonlight.

"Oh, look!" said I. "It's Minh and Quyan."

"Get away!" barked Sergeant Battle.

"But . . ." I protested, "They're my friends."

"No, they're not! They'd just as soon slaughter you as look at you. They only want money!"

He pushed a five toward Minh, who recoiled from it. He shoved the money into the pocket of Minh's shirt. Minh snatched the bill and threw it on the ground, spitting at it. He kicked it back toward the Sergeant, who, ignoring the outcome of his ploy, roughly grabbed me by the elbow and shoved me through the door.

"You'd better pack tonight," he snapped. "We leave at 0600 sharp!" Apparently, he too had taken a ride in an open-faced cyclo where he'd parted with some ill-gotten piasters. And could never forget it.

I lay heavily on the bed wishing for rapprochement, for diplomacy, for a moment of fellow-feeling, for a deep and decent meeting of souls, for a fresh new way of being . . . like Saladin retaking Jerusalem from the Crusaders. Rather than massacre all Christians down to the last man, woman and child as they had done to the Muslims, he'd offered safe passage. Ah . . . to be the bearer of safe passage.

I sank into sleep.

The next morning as I was hustled—guitar, duffle bag and all—onto a waiting transport truck, I spied Minh and Quyan out front. Their eyes glowed like birthday candles! I scrambled to claim a place on the bench by the back opening of the truck, so I'd be able to wave goodbye. Then we started to roll. Minh and

PART IV

Quyan ran after us while the truck slowly picked up speed. Finally depleted, they stopped and stood frozen in the middle of the road. I watched them grow smaller and smaller until we rounded a bend. And then they were gone.
    Forever.

IT ALL BEGAN WITH CHERRY SOUP

VIETNAM
(Intro to Mercenary Children)

I was a folksinger for the USO in Southeast Asia during the Vietnam war. I feel, in a sense, like a veteran of foreign wars.

I well remember holding an M-16 on my lap as we rode in an army jeep down the highway most notorious for ambush attack . . . the same highway on which an entire USO troupe had later perished. We flew, sometimes twice a day, in cargo planes at an altitude of 20,000ft.

Taking antiaircraft fire, landing strips where flattened mountain peaks.

We toured Korea, Japan, Thailand, the Philippines, and Vietnam. And I came to understand, in these places, that we had often been preceded by "bad-will ambassadors" whose behavior contaminated the quality of our experiences. In Tokyo, I was eager to try gourmet delicacies in an exclusive Japanese restaurant. My host was forced to negotiate fiercely in order to gain my entrance. Because, as he explained, the proprietors had learned through bitter repetition, that no matter what's offered on the menu, many Americans will insist on hamburger.

In Seoul, Korea, I was ashamed when the soldier who'd been assigned to drive us gunned the jeep through a group of pedestrians just to see them scatter like so many chickens.

But now we were in Vietnam. And we were given three days of rest and recreation in a glorious seaside Shangri-la called Nha Trang, whose pristine beaches were legendary. With proverbial green and mist-shrouded islands rising from a perfectly translucent, turquoise sea. In the evening the sails of Chinese junks in the harbor caught the colors of the sunset.

Well. The first day, I jumped into a bathing suit and plunged into the ocean. Whereupon I was immediately surrounded by a small gang of children bent on drowning me with vigorous splashing. Then one of them, a boy around seven or eight years old, separated from the pack and joined my team.

We frolicked in the waves most of the day. After that, we were pals. So we toured around town together, window shopping, eating exotic fruit and banana yogurt, and taking rides in cyclos, the bicycle-driven taxis. I spoke not one word of Vietnamese, and the only English he knew was, "You numbah one!" For three days, our entire conversation consisted of "You numbah one!" I recommend that kind of verbal diet. It boosts the immune system.

Anyway, on the last night of our stay, I was invited to dine with a group of Vietnamese officers. After a very French lobster dinner, I was astonished when each of these high-ranking military men, in turn, recited poetry and sang sweet-sounding Vietnamese songs. It was the most vivid example of the wide variety of cultural possibilities I'd encountered so far.

At the end of the evening, I returned to the hotel to find my little friend and his even smaller sister waiting for me. They were radiant! I stopped to exchange a volley of "you numbah one"s with them when we were interrupted by the billeting officer, a genuine anti-diplomat. Who, over my objections and explanations, was intent on proving that avarice, cunning and manipulation were the only forces that drove these children.

The following poem documents that event. It's a true story.

MERCENARY CHILDREN
In the style of a Georgia Sea Islands play-party song (to be read against a 2/3 polyrhythm).

They took me down to the water.
Day in, day out.
There was boats floatin' on the water.
Send them on home.

The sky and the water was the same color.
Day in, day out.
There was blood on the water.
Send them on home.

There was children playin' in the water.
Day in, day out.
And soldiers standin' on the seashore.
Send them on home.

The soldiers watch the games of the babies.
Day in, day out.
They say the children are the mercenaries.
Send them on home.

They say the children want your money.
Day in, day out.
They give the child the five dollar.
Send them on home.

The child throw the money on the water.
Day in, day out.
He spit on the dollar!
Send them on home.

PART IV

They took me down to the water.
Day in, day out.
There was blood on the water.
Send them on home.
Send them on home.

Send them on home!

THE CLASH OF FUNDAMENTALISMS

In the Clash of Fundamentalisms, it seems that those with the biggest, angriest, most punitive and warlike gods will win. In which case the gods of money and guns would most certainly have the advantage. Unless they encountered Ghandi. Because huge numbers of peace-loving resisters have always prevailed in the end. But the Clash of Fundamentalisms has made me think . . . What would it be like to worship a truly cruel god? Would it be like worshipping a schoolyard bully of a god who grows up to be a something like a menacing deep-cover CIA operative?

This offering is entitled "Ann Coulter in Paradise". or "My Least Favorite Being on The Planet".

My god is taller than your god.

My god challenges your god to an arm-wrestling contest and wins. By cheating.

During school prayer, my god looks the most angelic, and he prays the loudest. Later, he beats up your god on the playground.
Mom loves my god best. NAH-nah, nah-nah, NAH, nah.

My god dates your god's girlfriend. When she is great with child, he pretends he's never met her.

Wanna know the weirdest thing about my god? He would trade hundreds of thousands of grown human lives by way of starvation, bombing their nations, radiation, and electrocution for one tiny clump of undifferentiated cells.

My god requires a massive blood sacrifice in order to feel like a proper deity.

My god is a spoiled god.

Only those who specifically believe in my god and none other shall be admitted into heaven for close-order drill and K-rations in the eternal bunkers of paradise.

PART IV

Well, isn't this special!

My god has arranged for you to deliver all your material wealth to the Fortune 500, the Department of War, or ExxonMobil. Whoever is closest.

Because my god doesn't want your character ruined by handling filthy money. Isn't my god thoughtful?

Now that you're thoroughly impoverished, your god thinks my god will take care of you when you're too old to work. Ha ha ha ha ha! On your 65th birthday, my god sends you a degenerate greeting card, a six-pack of cat chow, and a bill for the federal deficit.

All day long my god utters high-sounding phrases about peace and loving kindness. But after midnight, my god slips through the keyhole of your god's apartment door for purposes of malicious mayhem.

My god drenches your gods heart and liver with ketchup, while catching fair and balanced reruns of Sean Hannity and Bill O'Reilly.

Later, my god turns your gods remains into head cheese and summer sausage and, just for a goof, invites Tony Blair in for lunch.

Mr. Blair thinks your god tastes just like chicken.

Did I mention that my god is a shapeshifter who sometimes assumes a female form? A truly evil female form.

Then things really get crazy when my girl god (aka Ann Coulter) dresses up in a fake mustache with a banana behind the zipper of her pants and goes dancing with Jerry Falwell.

She tickles his mouth with her lip hairs until he screams, "Auntie . . . Auntie Mame!" and blesses all the gay weddings at Disneyland.

She pierces his navel with a rhinestone stud and abandons him gibbering and goose-fleshed, waiting in pink satin briefs for her call.

Poor Jerry Falwell. He says he's never felt this way before. Poor, poor Jerry.

Mom still loves my god best.

My god is the coolest god. Coolest or cruelest? Hmm. Oh Well.

My God is bigger than you.

THE GOLDMINER MANIFESTO
Good evening. Linda Albertano was unable to be with us tonight, so I'm appearing in her place. I'm Sugar Reynolds, editor of GOLDMINER MAGAZINE. GOLDMINER, the magazine for ambitious women, is a hybrid of Playboy and Forbes. It's an iconoclastic neo-feminist political philosophy. It's a state of mind that can be achieved only by concentrating on Bill Gates' annual income and multiplying by two.

1) We are Goldminers!
   We believe that the orderly transfer of wealth from the male sector to the female sector can be achieved through corporate sabotage, palimony, and stealth. Secrets slip from love-drunk lips!

2) We are Goldminers!
   Our weapons are fear, surprise, and massive settlements of divorce! Every dollar earned in court by the ex-Mrs. Johnny Carson adds a dollar to the economic weight of women as whole.

3) We are Goldminers!
   We spit on the concept of equal wages for equal work! We're dedicated to the proposition that we have an inalienable right to earn twice as much dough for our labors as they do for theirs! Let the pendulum swing in our direction for a few hundred years before centering. Then, on our cross-country flights, we'll be nurtured by perky, smiling stewards, catering to our every whim. And the buff bodies of nubile boys draped across the hoods of sexy roadsters in magazine auto ads will make our credit cards throb with unquenchable joy!

4) We are Goldminers!
   We believe that a man's erotic charms are most provocatively displayed when he's photographed naked on a bed of gold bullion revealing those twin parts of himself so alluring to women——the weight of his net worth and the net worth of his weight. Think of Bill Gates' annual income and multiply by two. Picture Donald Trump

with a staple through his navel. You're almost there. You're very close to a state of perfect Goldminer!

5) We are Goldminers!
We assert that beauty queens, movie starlets, and those women heretofore known to an ignorant and vulnerable public only as "bimbos" are on the front lines in a guerrilla war being waged surreptitiously against select members of the privileged gender. You will meet our lieutenants in pricey little fern bars. In the cushioned hallways of your executive suites. On the casting couches of your television evangelists.

6) We are Goldminers!
Gennifer Flowers is the captain of our Drill Team! Monica Lewinsky is replacing Jerry Springer. Linda Tripp is buying an island in the Bahamas and using your reputation for collateral.
Just give her a new tape recorder, 50 million dollars and unlimited time to and I'm sure she can find something you won't want posted all over the internet!
But . . . . The second Mrs. Stallone still holds the crown for Goldminer of the century by divesting Sylvester of 6 million large ones in record time!

WE ARE GOLDMINERS!
Ah, Ha Ha Ha Ha Ha Ha Ha Ha Ha Ha Ha Ha Ha

PART V
POEMS BY FRANK LUTZ

NOT FORGOTTEN DAD

Sometimes
when I'm alone
and thinking about him
as a young man
in college
an athlete and
a scholar
in the 1920's
in Wisconsin
near the lakes
the wistful words
of the old Wiffenpoof Song
come to mind.

"To the tables down at Maurie's . . ."

We hear about
the gaiety
of that era
but I believe
it was different.
I see
in my mind's eye
autumn leaves falling on a melancholy
late afternoon
with the long
yellow and orange rays of the northern sun in a pale blue sky bringing quiet
to life all around.

"To the place where Louie dwells . . ."

I picture
a boarding house all wood and brick
rich in the colors
of the times,
a place
for young men
in letter-sweaters
to live
and I see him
coming down the stairs
books in hand
leaning on the banister touching the round knob on top of
the bottom post
as he swings
from the last step
to the floor.

"Gentlemen songsters off on a spree . . ."

He stops and looks
across the hall
through the living room
and out the window
smiling
to see
the long rays
of the afternoon sun
and wonders
in the quiet
about his future.

"Doomed from here to eternity . . ."

In forty years he will have
survived the Depression
been to war
met Mom
settled down
had three children
loved them all
got them started
and then
while not yet an old man
died.

"Oh Lord have mercy on such as we . . ."

But for now
the strains
of the old college song
keep him there
in a simpler time
when he is young
the world is innocent
and he can ponder
what it all must
have been like
for his own
Dad.

"And we will pass and be forgotten with the rest."

THE KING

I lay in bed one night
In the soft candle light
Coming from across the room.
Because I was with another she
My nocturnal world turned out to be
Filled with feelings of gloom.

I slowly drifted off
She beside me was asleep and soft
But my sleep was restless and disturbed.
My dream began to unfold
Into a story to be told
That would leave me ever more perturbed.

In my cloud of restless sleep
The quiet would not keep
As my vision brought the new dawn.
The King beside his Queen
Lay in bed unable to dream
As he heard outside footsteps closer drawn.

A loud knock on the cabin door
Up bolted the King to cross the floor
Donning his robe and jeweled crown.
To the portal with sword in hand
Unlatched it slowly, on guard, and
Outside stood three noblemen in the misty dawn.

"We've come to take your Queen,"
One said, showing courage and spleen,
"You've not proved your right to her."
Without a word this great King
Stepped out and motioned them to the ring
Of oaks some yards distant but not far.

"I'll take you one on one," he said.
"And may the loser lose his head.
But if you attack me all together
I may lose the fight and die
But two of you will join me nie
And the third will have lost his honor forever."

The first approached to fight,
Attacked with all his might
But soon died in great pain.
The second had fought before
And with his arms could score,
But the King soon counted victims twain.

The third said, "You are hurt,
Bleeding, tired and even worse,
Have met your maker this grim day."
The fight did not last long
And before the first bird's song
A third nobleman was put to the lay.

The King was glad he'd won
But sad at what he'd done
Although the fight had taken its toll.
"These big men were warriors great.
Oh, it's what I dearly hate
To fight with those I should love, all."

Hurt and cut but tall and stately
He returned from where he'd been lately.
Disrobed and quietly got back in bed.
His Queen who beside him did lie
Pretended sleep with a tear in her eye.
He kissed her cheek and lay down his weary head.

As the King started to dream deep
I awoke from my sleep,
It was still the middle of the night.
The lady beside me was not the same
As the fabled Queen who was my flame
And for whom in any age I'd fight.

Lovers, just remember this,
There's no such thing as eternal bliss,
Get that notion out of your head.
So when you get the urge to roam
Go get your true Queen at home
And take her to her own King's bed!

TO DALTON TRUMBO –
FROM A WOUNDED SOLDIER.

Waking, lying on
my side,
with one eye open,
I feel still
like I always do
when I first wake up.
Staring out from bed
all is white
like the sheets
and in the blurry distance
what seems to be the wall.

Early mornings in summer
when I'd stir on my side
from my sleep
and look out through the window
I'd see from my bed
with just one eye open
blue sky
trees
green grass
hollyhocks against the barn
red and white
and peonies in a bed
all white.

I feel the gentle touch
of a hand on
my hip.
Is it Mom
or Dad
waking me from

a bad dream?
Early summer mornings
she'd be
the first one up and
her voice
would drone
in sleepy tones
in the background
as she told the others
to let me
sleep.

Now I feel
another touch
but I also feel
a pinprick
or sting
in my hip.
Is it Mom?
or Dad?
In the background
I hear dull voices
almost muted.

Wish
I could hear
what they
say.

Should get up but I'm
too stiff and tired.
Maybe Mom will let me sleep
a little longer
like she usually does.
I should turn on my other side

and look out the window
at the flowers.
Wish I could turn over.
Why can't I turn over?

Funny, but I'm looking
out of my bottom eye
and the top one seems
to be shut
or covered with something.
I'll reach up and
uncover it—
oh, well, maybe later,
seems too hard to move
just now.

Some other time,
some other place,
in a field
it seems like I
stepped on
a loud boom,
later friendly hands
picked me up,
voices yelling urgently.
The booms,
the sound of gunfire
and cannon
near me.
Then quiet.

Wonder how long
I've been sleeping
on this side.
Seems like a long time

since summer mornings
at home,
but I could have sworn
I heard Mom's voice
in the background.
Wonder why she doesn't
come talk to me
or try to make me get up.

Looks like a hand
in front of my eye
and something gold
and shiny
like a star
being put on the sheet
by my head.
Somebody just touched
my head.
Was that you, Mom?

D-DAY, NORMANDY – JUNE 6, 1944

Do we cry for them
still?
See the photos.
See the films.
Who they were,
what they did there,
magnificent.

Does anybody cry for them
still?
One was your father,
or your grandfather.
You in the future
look back at your ancestors.
Look at their young faces,
learn what they did.
Magnificent.

Find them in Europe
or in the Pacific.
Wherever they went
they changed it all,
made the war end,
made it all better
for us.

Don't forget them
ever.
If to remember them
and what they did
brings tears to your eyes,
then cry for them
still.

LANCASTERS OVER CANADA

We left Butte
and Anaconda copper
just at cold blue dawn,
climbed out between the clouds
stayed a few hundred feet
above the mountain tops
and pines,
light snow already in early autumn,
elk running,
saw Tee-pees below
and serpentine rivers flow
as we flew on north
to Canada.
Many miles turned great hills
into flat lands,
magnificent vistas,
huge bluffs and buffalo-runs,
pasture lands.
Landed on a short strip
called Choteau
in the middle of
vast wheat fields
laid bare for winter
in long even lines
like grooves on a brown board,
rectangular patterns from the sky,
the symmetry of it all
like artwork done
by the hand of
God.
Flew on past the mountains where
old Chief Sitting Bull
hid out from the

U.S. Army,
and later three Canadian Mounties
turned him over to
a whole Regiment
of our scared soldiers.
Just past Lethbridge
Loyd said looking left
and pointing down
"An old abandoned
R.C.A.F. base
left from
World War II
where they trained
our boys
to fly Lancasters.
Can you imagine
landing a Lancaster
on such a short dirt strip?"

No, I couldn't,
and I thought
of all the ghosts
from forty-plus years ago
still sitting below us
in those classrooms
learning about
instrument navigation,
emergency procedures,
fire in the cockpit,
bomb sighting,
the final run into the enemy target.
Young men who never returned
once had walked
down below us
from the sortie room

over to the main hangar
for a cup of hot coffee
in the Canadian cold
then out to the taxiway
in winter weather
to kick the tires
and light the fires
of their Lancasters.
Then one day
it was over
and they headed east
to England.
Caught a ride across the pond
with their Yankee pals
in their Flying Fortresses
to rendezvous on
King John's ancient island
set in a silver sea
and flew their Lancasters again
but this time
not over the peaceful plains
of Western Canada
with the Rockies
out their windows
but over Deutschland
with Bf 109s
out their windows
trying to shoot them
from the skies.
Everything they'd learned
was tested
only this time
if they failed the test
it all ended
in flames.

Snapping back
to here and now
we landed at a dirt strip
just outside Calgary
with the ghosts of our fathers' generation
miles behind us
in the old aerodrome.
We left them there,
in that
holy
place.

PERUGIAN SOULS

So many souls have walked the streets of this old
    town at night.
And all the holes within her walls have eyes that
    watch the sights.
Now I alone surround myself with dark and misty
    air,
The ancient stones beneath my feet are marked by who
    was there.

The city sleeps, the stars keep watch, and I can feel
    the eyes,
Watching me creep out in the dark, as I listen for bye-
    gone sighs.
The voices speak to me quite plain and leave me struck
    aghast,
My feelings peek when I hear tales of the grand Italian
    past.

Great Caesar's men marched through these streets on their
    way to Gaul,
And Popes knew when this land was theirs to take and
    rule it all.
Great art is here for one to see in every arch
    and street,
But I hold most dear those long dead souls out in the night
    I meet.

RENAISSANCE NIGHT

Warm breezes blow while soft lights glow
From rooms in the Italian town.
As I recline I see the shine
As night-shades are pulled down.

While she sleeps my mind keeps
A pace with thoughts of the past.
In this ancient town where ghosts abound
And the sounds of life still last.

With different names we're all the same
As those who were here before.
We shed our clothes as the warm wind blows,
Leave open the windows and door.

From my bed as I turn my head
I can see and smell the trees.
I blow out the light in this Renaissance night
And say my prayers on my knees.

My sword hangs there on the back of a chair,
My shirt lies on top of her dress.
I feel soft wind across my skin
And she nods as she feels my caress.

At night I can see as they beckon to me
Images from a long time ago.
I know I've been there, I know just where,
And it's back I'd like to go.

But I'm here now and I know just how
And when I can take flight.
I'll live the way that I do by day
So I can dream in my Renaissance night.

PART VI
STORIES BY FRANK LUTZ

CARMEN IN THE KREMLIN

It was late afternoon in October in Moscow. The sky was dark, the day was cold, with snow flurries. The sky is always dark late in the afternoon in October in Moscow. If you look on a world map you can see why. It's farther north than New York City or Montreal, or even Copenhagen.

My pal Carmen and I were late getting to the Kremlin. We wanted to see the famous Kremlin Museum before we left Moscow. It was like a dream come true to be here at this ancient fortress of the Czars of Russia. We were walking fast across the Kremlin moat toward the museum with our guide, a local girl named Lena. She was tall and beautiful. It turns out that Moscow has a lot of tall and beautiful young women, a state secret that Russian men keep to themselves when they travel abroad, for obvious reasons. And a lot of these gorgeous women are named Lena. This Lena was a secretary in the employ of our good friend Reed. He was generous enough to loan her to us for a few days, to escort us around Moscow to see all of the cultural attractions. Carmen and I needed culture. In fact, we still need culture. I hope someday it improves us.

As the three of us were bundling ourselves against the cold, we came up to the main outside entrance to the museum. A sign said the museum would be closing in fifteen minutes. Through the doors and inside, in the main lobby, there was a long line-up ahead of us of about fifty cute little Russian school kids. They were there with their teachers to see the museum. They seemed to be between six and eight years old, all with blond hair and rosy little cheeks and cold hands. They were holding each other's hands to stay in line and rubbing their hands to keep them warm as they stood there, waiting to see the museum. They start early to give their kids culture in Russia. Wish they had started earlier with Carmen and me. It would have done us a lot of good.

There was a log-jam in the procession of children trying to enter the museum. Everything was at a standstill. At the front of the line the teachers were going over a stack of papers with the old lady in charge of selling admission tickets to the museum. She was seated at a desk behind a window, and she was definitely in charge. She was one of the famous Russian "Babuschkas". A Babuschka is a Russian grandmother. But she's more than a grandmother. The Babuschkas run Russia. Yeltsin thinks he does. The new Russian Congress thinks they do. But everybody knows that Babuschkas run Russia, because they control the doors to enter buildings all over Russia. Apartment buildings. State buildings. The Congress buildings. Department stores. Train stations. On and on. And if they don't want to let you in, they won't open the door. So if the Babuschka at the door to the Kremlin gets mad at Yeltsin because the economy is bad, she just refuses to open the door, he can't get in, and everything stops. The lesson is, you must treat Babuschka very gently, with great respect.

I had been in Moscow for a couple of weeks, staying in one of Reed's apartments in one of the thousands of huge apartment buildings in Moscow, which is a city of apartment buildings. You don't see individual houses in Moscow. Just large office buildings, state buildings, and apartment buildings. Even so, it has a lot of old and elegant architecture, and is a very pretty city.

Downstairs inside the entrance hall in each of these apartment buildings sits a Babuschka in a little enclosed office, with a window in it. She sees, or monitors, everyone who comes in or goes out. Babuschka is ever watchful, on duty twenty-four hours a day.

The entrance doors to the apartment buildings have a push-button code-lock system. To activate it, you press several buttons in a code, then a buzzer button, which unlocks the door automatically. Easy. I had been doing this several times a day for two weeks, as I came in and out of Reed's apartment. And always I would greet Babuschka in Russian with "Good morning" or "Good day" or "Good evening." And she would always greet me back in the same fashion, adding "Thank you" in Russian.

Then late one night it was very cold and snowing outside. I could not find a taxi, so I hitchhiked from a restaurant back to the apartment. I had negotiated a good price with the driver, who was a privateer taxi driver. A lot of Moscow motorists do this, in order to get a little extra gas money. But by the time I got back to the apartment building I was still cold from being outside for so long looking for a ride. So I was anxious to get inside to Reed's apartment.

I approached the entrance door to the building and pressed all of the buttons, then the buzzer. Nothing happened! I did the routine again—nothing! It was late, I was freezing, and was starting to panic. I had read history books about all of those soldiers with Napoleon, and later Hitler, freezing to death in the cold Russian winter. Now it was going to happen to me!

I started pounding on the door. After a couple of minutes, I heard a little old lady's voice say to me in Russian through the door:

"Who are you?"

It was Babuschka. She was doing a security check. I had heard about these security checks, done spontaneously at the complete whim of Babuschka. If I didn't answer correctly, she could leave me out in the cold to freeze to death! I decided to remain calm. In Russian I answered her:

"It's me, the American, staying in number eleven."

"What do you want?"

"I want to come inside."

"Why are you here?"

At this point the cold got to me. The calm left me. I began laughing at the ridiculousness of my situation. Here I was, about to freeze to death in Russia, far from my homeland. And I wasn't even going to die as a hero in the service of my country in some foreign war. Instead, I was being done-in by a little old Babuschka who didn't want to open the door. And the irony was—she knew me! She would say "Hello" to me every day and every night for two weeks! But now, she was going to let me die in the Russian winter, just like one of Napoleon's soldiers!

I was laughing uncontrollably, when suddenly the door opened, just a crack. I could see that it was Babuschka, peering out at me, with a puzzled look on her face as if to say, "Why are you laughing? This is serious business!"

The only thing I could think to do was to say "Good evening. See, it's me, the American" in Russian. I did this, at which point she said "Da"—yes—and opened the door for me.

I entered, said "Good evening" again, and she replied in kind, along with her usual "Thank you.". I walked up to the apartment and went to bed.

But now here I was at the Kremlin Museum with Carmen and Lena, and it was about to close. In control of the situation was Babuschka. I had to see what the problem was, so I asked Lena to investigate.

After a couple of minutes Lena came back to me and explained.

"Frank, it seems that all of these children have to be checked in by Babuschka. She has to have the name of each child on a separate piece of paper, one paper for each one child. Then she has to verify that each child is here, according to papers. Like for security. Maybe they are afraid these sweet little children will steal Kremlin treasures. It is typical bureaucratic mess. Ridiculous."

One must understand that in Mother Russia to have a good job like Babuschka's, guarding the artifacts in the Kremlin Museum, is more than just a job. It is a mission, a holy trust.

I had to think fast because time was wasting. Luckily, Carmen had brought with him several of his army medals from when he was a soldier during World War II, fighting in Europe. The medals were impressive, but normally he didn't wear them in public, except for special occasions. But he always carried them in his coat pocket in case of an emergency, such as if he might have to impress somebody. In Russia, people are impressed by decorated veterans who have a lot of medals, and this was an emergency. And I noticed that Babuschka was wearing medals, too. Maybe she was a veteran of the Great Patriotic War, what we call World War II. If so, maybe she would sympathize with us when she saw Carmen's medals.

I told Carmen:

"Listen, man. Get all of the medals out of your pocket and put them on. Like now. And look really proud. I've got a plan."

Carmen quickly went into action. Then I took Lena by the arm.

"Lena, here's what I want you to do. Carmen is putting on his war medals. When he has done that, I want you to take him by the arm, and walk him up to the front of the line, in front of everybody. I want you to take him up to Babuschka and tell her that Carmen is a Hero of the Great Patriotic War. That he fought during the war here in Europe to free his Russian comrades from the Nazis. That he was wounded four times, and that he won many medals, among them the Bronze Star for heroism and valor. Tell her that Carmen has never seen the Kremlin Museum, and that he has come all the way from California with me, his nephew, to see it. And that he must return to America tomorrow, so he may never again have a chance to see this museum."

By the time I finished my speech, Lena was inspired. She did exactly as I told her to do. I stood behind the two of them and watched Babuschka's face. As Lena went through her routine, I noticed that Babuschka's face did not change. No expression. No emotion. Tough, hard and cold, like the Russian winter. Perhaps she was a former member of the KGB?

Finally, as Lena was finishing her speech, she put her arm around Carmen's shoulder. I could hear her soft voice rise, and her tone became more emotional. Carmen slumped a little now, making himself look old, tired and sad, with a pitiful look on his face. With one hand, he was pointing to the medals on his chest. It was a scene that would melt the coldest, hardest heart. Would it melt Babuschka's?

Then Lena stopped talking. Everybody in the hall was now quiet—the guards, the teachers, the kids.

Babuschka looked at Carmen. She looked at the medals on his chest. She looked at me. She looked at Lena. Then suddenly, with a grand, wide, sweeping gesture of her arm she motioned us forward, toward the guards at the entrance into the main wing of the museum. She looked at the guards.

"Let them in!" she cried. "No charge!"

It was great.

CARMEN AND THE C-NOTE

Jimmy Cerritos is a big guy. Especially for an Italian-American. I mean, I'm a big guy, and tall. But Jimmy is as big as I am. He has huge hands. He uses them mostly for typing. Home for Jimmy is in the far north of America. Buffalo, New York, where he spends the Arctic winters holed up in his apartment, reading and typing. That's what he likes about Buffalo. In the winter it's too cold outside to do anything, so he gets to stay inside and work on his stuff. Short stories, poems, articles on military history, even a novel. He only goes out to teach part-time at the local university.

Jimmy is an ex-U.S. Marine, trained for combat during the Vietnam War era. He's proud of his Marine Corps decorations and of his battle scars. But in lieu of Vietnamese bullet wounds, the marks on his body are from fights he's had with drunk Marines or civilians stupid enough to take him on. I would use better sense . . . Yes, Jimmy is a colorful person, an interesting mix, part brawler, part intellectual. He is not unlike many famous writers and poets of bygone eras who have walked on the tough side of the streets. Jean Genet, François Villon, Christopher Marlowe, to name a few, were equally great as writers and as street fighters. Perhaps some of the same passions that drive the poet also drive the fighter. So it must be with Jimmy.

In the summertime Jimmy loves to come to Los Angeles. His parents live in LA, so that's his excuse. But what he really likes to do in LA is work in Carmen's Hollywood restaurant in the evenings as the bartender. Carmen's restaurant has been there in Hollywood as a popular Italian food place since shortly after World War II ended. Carmen came out to LA from his native Chicago just after his release from the U.S. Army because, to quote him, "that place was just too damned cold in winter." He almost froze to death late one winter night in Chicago after he'd missed the last train home. The next day he packed his clothes, kissed his mother goodbye and headed west. He's lived in LA ever since.

IT ALL BEGAN WITH CHERRY SOUP

At the time of our story, about forty years after the end of World War II, Carmen has several successful restaurants in the LA area. Places where people like to bring their children to show them and say, "This is where your mom and I used to go for dinner when we were dating, before we got married and had you." Now in some cases their children are bringing the grandchildren and saying, "This is where Grandma and Grandpa used to come for dinner when they were dating." The charm of it all stays in the families like that.

Now it was a hot Saturday evening in July, after the sun had gone down. Summers in LA can get beastly, and Carmen's Hollywood restaurant is a good place to have a drink and cool off before dinner. The windows in the upstairs bar were opened to the street. The place was packed with people having a good time. Jazz music was coming from the corner where the combo was playing in their shirtsleeves. The bar created a romance of its own. The air smelled of perfume and booze, mixed with the aroma of garlic and wine from the food. There was not much smoke in the place—this was, after all, Southern California, where nobody smokes much. And the ambiance was definitely romantic.

It was on nights such as this that Carmen would remind me that he and his buddies had won the war in Europe some forty years before, so that forty-some years later my buddies and I would be able to enjoy nights like this in America. I could never argue the point with him. Carmen Miceli was a bona fide World War II combat soldier and hero, in my eyes. As a platoon Sergeant deployed to the Battle of Normandy, he was wounded four times as he fought his way across France, Belgium, Holland, and finally into Deutschland. But more than that, he was decorated with the Bronze Star, one of our nation's highest awards for bravery on the battlefield, for neutralizing a German machine gun nest and rescuing three of his outfit buddies while under enemy fire. He was decorated by the great General George Patton during a full-dress ceremony with hundreds of his fellow soldiers in attendance. I have seen the photos on the front page of the U.S. Military's Stars and Stripes newspaper of the time, June 1944.

This Saturday night Jimmy Cerritos was working the bar when I showed up. The place was very crowded, and I did not want to take up space sitting on a bar stool. I preferred to leave space for the paying customers, as I was there only to say hello and chat with Jimmy for a few minutes. Since I was an old pal of Carmen's and knew well the workings of his restaurants, I was allowed to go behind the bar, which I did. I could talk with Jimmy as he worked. We both liked it that way, Jimmy and I, as we could see eye-to-eye easier, due to our respective sizes. And occasionally I would help out by pouring a drink for a customer.

Between customer demands, and even above the din of the crowd and the high decibel levels of the music, Jimmy and I were carrying on a running dialogue about Operation Barbarossa, Hitler's attack on Russia early in the morning of Sunday, June 21, 1941, thus betraying Stalin and starting the war on the Eastern Front. To this day the Russians call it the Great Patriotic War, while we call it World War II.

Jimmy was rattling on about the German Army Groups North, Central and South. "It was brilliant!" he would say. "The Germans had it all figured out, but with one fatal flaw. As winter approached, some Wehrmacht clerk, some lowly Corporal in the German Army back in Berlin, screwed up. On a requisition sheet for uniforms, he put a checkmark in the wrong column, and the summer uniforms went to Russia, and the winter uniforms went to Africa, just the opposite of where they were needed and supposed to go. As a consequence, thousands of German troops would freeze to death in Russia before the right uniforms could be sent to them."

Just then we noticed Carmen walking up the steps from the restaurant to the bar. He was dressed elegantly and looked like a don. People greeted him, he shook hands, kissed ladies' hands, addressed the ladies as "dahling" or "dear" regardless of age, touched kids on their heads. He was a great public relations man, a smooth operator, like Bogie in *Casablanca.*

There was a break in the music as Carmen approached the service end of the bar, where Jimmy and I were standing. We greeted him from behind the bar, and he ordered his usual scotch on the rocks.

"How's it going, guys?" he asked us.

"It's going great, Carmen! Lots of excitement tonight! Just look at this crowd!" Jimmy answered.

"Jimmy was just telling me about the German clerk who screwed up and sent the uniforms to the wrong places during Operation Barbarossa, Carm," I said.

"Oh, yeah," he said. "That guy really screwed up. What'd the Germans do with him after that fiasco, Jimmy? Shoot him, or what?"

"Dunno, Carm. It's not in the books anywhere. I imagine the guy did his best to disappear, once he realized what he'd done. Or maybe he spent his last days fighting on the Russian Front."

We all laughed a fearful, nervous laugh at the prospect of fighting and freezing to death on the Russian Front in the winter of 1941.

As Jimmy was replying to Carmen in more detail about the war in Russia, Augostino the waiter walked up to the service end of the bar beside Carmen to order drinks for one of his tables. "Augie", as he was known to us all, was from Mexico, and had been with Carmen for over twenty-five years, as a waiter. During that time, he had got married, had a family, raised all his kids, and helped send them to college, and now had grandchildren. All the while working as a waiter for Carmen. And no matter what, no matter how slow business might become in bad times, Carmen could never think of firing Augie or anybody else who had been with him for so long. So Augie had job security for the rest of his days, whether he knew it or not.

Augie didn't talk much, but was always respectful and friendly, and always glad to see Carmen. After they'd greeted each other, Carmen's voice rose a little as he spoke to Augie in a demanding voice.

"Tell me something, Augie. Have you sold any drinks tonight?"

"Yes, sir, sure have."

"How many?"

"Well, I don't know for sure."

"Are you satisfied with how many drinks you've sold tonight, Augie?"

Now Carmen's voice was getting louder. As it did, the crowd started getting quieter. They were beginning to look in Carmen's direction, paying attention to what was going on between Augie and him. Carmen's baritone voice was commanding their attention. Jimmy and I were watching, too, as we were standing right in front of the boss and his employee, watching from our vantage point on the other side of the bar.

"Oh, well, I guess I could sell some more drinks, Mr. Miceli."

By this time Carmen had taken a new, crisp one-hundred-dollar bill out of his pants pocket, a C-Note. He had unfolded it to full length, and held it up with his thumb and forefinger, in front of Augie's face. Of course, the whole crowd could see what was going on with the C-Note. In a raised voice Carmen asked:

"Augie, what is this, can you tell me?"

"Yes, sir. It's a one-hundred-dollar bill."

"Right! A C-Note! One hundred dollars!"

Now everybody in the bar was involved. They all had their eyes on the C- Note in Carmen's hand. At this point, with a grand gesture, Carmen stuffed the C-Note into Augie's jacket pocket. With a drill sergeant's authority he admonished the startled waiter:

"Now, Augie, go out and sell some more drinks!"

"Yes, sir, Mr. Miceli!"

The crowd was spellbound. Jimmy and I were astonished. And Augie's eyes were as big a pizza platter. Carmen had just laid a one-hundred-dollar tip on Augie, just in order to get him to sell some more drinks. One hundred dollars in those days was more than twice as much as Augie's wages for an eight-hour day. One hundred dollars was a full night's tips on a great night. One hundred dollars in the early '80s was still a lot of money, especially for just standing there answering questions for your boss. Boy, were we impressed!

Carmen finished his drink and greeted a few other people in the barroom area. Then he left. For the rest of the evening, and for several evenings thereafter, the main topic of conversation among the regulars was the tip. Conversations like: "Did you see what Carmen did tonight? Laid one hundred dollars on Augie—just like that! A C-Note tip, just to get him to sell some more drinks. What an incentive program. Maybe I should get a job here, too!"

That evening, I went home and told Linda about the C-Note tip. For the next few weeks my conversations with Jimmy always included talk of the C-Note tip. We did a play-by-play review of events leading up to the tip. The employees were still talking about it, too. Carmen was definitely big-time in everybody's eyes.

Several weeks later Carmen and I had occasion to lunch together at Musso-Franck's Restaurant on Hollywood Boulevard. As we talked, I mentioned to him the C-Note tip.

"That was an electric moment, Carmen, when you gave Augie the hundred-dollar tip. Everybody was impressed. Even Jimmy and I were impressed."

Carmen looked across our table straight at me with that "now you're gonna learn something, kid" look of his on his face. Waving his fork in his hand he said:

"So you guys liked that, huh? Thought that was pretty impressive, huh?"

"Yeah, well, a hundred bucks is a lot of dough."

"Well, do you wanna know the real story behind the hundred dollars? I mean, the truth about the C-Note? The origin of that C-Note tip, and why I gave it to Augie?"

"Hell yes, I mean, yeah, I thought that was just a big tip you were giving him, to sell more drinks. Was there something else going on?" I was dying of curiosity.

"Well, the truth of the matter is, a few weeks before that, I was down in the restaurant one night and I was broke, so I borrowed a hundred bucks from Augie. So the night you guys thought I was giving him a C-Note tip, I was really just paying him back. That's all. Simple as that."

He then smiled at me with a twinkle in his eye and looked down and calmly continued eating his lunch, osso-bucco, his favorite dish. We both knew at that moment that the C-Note story was, for us, over, fini. It had had its desired effect, or the effect Carmen wanted, that is: the event had got people excited. People would relive and retell the details of Carmen questioning Augie; the C-Note held up in front of Augie's eyes; the flourish with which Carmen would stuff the C-Note into Augie's pocket; Augie's eyes wide open with surprise. The drama of the event would live on for others in its mythology. But for us the truth of it had ended it with dramatic resolution. Now Carmen could talk about other things. So as he ate, he started talking about other things.

I was struck dumb by this news. So was Jimmy when I told him.

But we never told anybody else.

LA FRITTATA

It was a very warm day. It was Italy, and it was springtime.

The overwhelming beauty of that place has been told by natives and visitors alike throughout the centuries. And here it was, in all its verdant beauty. High hills and valleys all run together in a long peninsula sticking out into the blue Mediterranean Sea. The florid colors of it, the greens and reds, yellows and blues, the pastoral wonderland interrupted occasionally by ancient hillside towns made of sandstone and granite and marble. It feels always of art and music and poetry.

He was seated high above the street, via U. Rocchi, at a table on a portico, an open-air porch with a roof over it, the roof supported by weathered marble columns. The portico, the columns, the entire building were centuries old. The ancient building was situated on the downslope of a city hill, at the corner where via U. Rocchi meets the via Pinturicchio. The building is adjacent to, and helps to support on one side, the even older Arco Etrusco, an arch built high up and over the street, into the city wall several hundred years before the life of Christ by the pre-historic people known as the Etruscans. They were the people who invented the keystone arch, the strongest type of arch, that supplanted the old column and lintel structure that was used in wall openings or doors, such as one sees at the ancient city of Memphis in Egypt, or at earlier Stone Henge, or even in modern house construction today, over windows and doors. The keystone arch is capable of supporting much more weight than the column and lintel construction. It is also, in the minds of many people, a much more beautiful and elegant structure.

So here he was, fifty feet or so above the streets below, a dizzying height when looking over the low wall of the portico and straight down. This building built into the city wall of Perugia, capital of the Region of Umbria in central Italy, was on the edge of town. The great city wall had for centuries been the protective town limits on all sides of the hill that housed the settlement of its people, within the confines of the wall. He was seated on the building's portico in the shade of its roof, waiting for his midday meal. He had just come from his classes at the university, a short walk away, and he had about two hours before the afternoon session. As he sat at table and looked out beyond the edges of the portico, beyond the downslope of the hill, the Umbrian countryside was spread out before him in the distance, breathtaking in its medieval beauty. A mix of low hills and green valleys, well cultivated fields of early grain, deciduous forests here and rows of tall, peaked Italian poplar trees over there, the occasional single standing pine tree, almond groves, olive trees, vineyards, farm animals in the fields, tile-roofed farmhouses built of stone. This was not the Middle Ages, but to the young American student it was transformative.

On the portico were some other tables where students were seated. It was a quiet time, as they all were caught up in the beauty of the near and distant scene before them, the panoramic Umbrian countryside. Behind them, a large door led from the open portico into the building and its great stone interior walls. Housed on this storey of the building high above street level was a pensione, a reasonably priced boarding house typical of Italy, where the monthly fee for accommodations included a room and linen service for the bed, with maid service, and two meals per day, breakfast and midday. It was home mainly to a few students and visiting professors. It was well run by three women: Anna and Maria, sisters in their early thirties, and their mother, Mamma, about twenty years older. They provided all of the services, including cooking, for their Pensione Arco Etrusco.

It was early in the school term, but the students had already settled into a daily routine: classes in the morning until about noon, then a two-hour lunch break, followed by a walk—passeggiata—up the hill of via U. Rocchi to the center of town with friends and back down again. Maybe a stop for a cold, tasty gelato on the way. Classes resumed at two o'clock and ended at four in the afternoon. The midday meal was always a welcome adventure, as the Italian cuisine was enjoyed by most students as one of the wonders of the world. Students had come to Perugia from all corners of the world, with widely varying habitual tastes in food, but Mamma and her daughters knew how to light up the eyes of the students under their care. Their culinary preparations looked as good as they tasted, and the aroma of various herbs and spices used in their food preceded the dishes coming out of the kitchen, like a beam of goodness finding its way to and caressing the young noses. And the bread, oh, the bread! Handmade and fresh-baked every morning in their great stone kitchen and ancient wood fired oven. The line from the Lord's Prayer, "Give us this day our daily bread," on the lips of the students became a mantric utterance, an expression of desire for the sublime flavor of Mamma's fresh bread.

This day would be another day of anticipation, a sort of gleeful state of mind, as students waited for the midday meal to be served. He was sitting alone at his table, as he had been reading, going over the verb forms Professor Barratti had taught them that morning. If twenty or so diners could be seated at any one time, given the number of tables on the portico, then only a few of them had yet arrived, so they could leave him to his reading as there were other empty tables available. He could feel Anna approaching him from behind, she was the sister who usually served diners on the portico. Her first gift to him would be some of the morning's fresh bread, and a small open mini carafe of virgin olive oil from the nearby Umbrian farms, from their olive trees. His mind was drawn away from his studies, as this was no ordinary olive oil, like what one might find in local markets in a big city. This was the real thing, cloudy and unfiltered, the fresh smell of flowers and a faint hint of young grass, sweet to the taste. It was perfect on anything it touched, whether bread, vegetables, salad, fruit, whatever. It replaced butter, the dairy favorite companion to bread all over North America. He pulled a saucer dish across the tablecloth to a spot in front of him. From the carafe he poured about two tablespoons of olive oil onto the saucer dish. Finely ground fresh black pepper was in a small, uncovered ramekin dish on the table. He took a pinch of it and dropped it into the olive oil. Now it was ready for bread dipping, a favorite taste treat while he waited for the main dish to come from Mamma's kitchen.

The meal Anna placed before him next would have a profound effect on his own culinary sensibilities for decades to come. It was unlike anything he had tasted before that day. It was something Anna called La Frittata, an egg dish prepared in kitchens throughout Italy, but this would be his first time to taste it. This Midwesterner from Ohio had grown up in a cosmopolitan family of well-travelled parents and relatives. He himself, young though he was, had already travelled to five continents, and had experienced exotic foods, and had developed a cultivated love of regional cooking. Indeed, his parents had been like that, experimental and accepting of many food styles. In his home he had tasted many egg dishes, including omelets with various fillings, eggs Benedict, Mexican spiced eggs. He had eaten Quiche Lorraine and soufflés in France, eggs Biryani in India, Huevos Rancheros in Mexico, coddled eggs in London. But La Frittata was a complete surprise to him, at first unrecognized by him as an egg dish.

Anna first placed before him a demi-carafe of a local light bodied white table wine, cooled somewhat to counter the warmth of the day. On request, it could be watered down a bit, to prevent drowsiness during the afternoon's activities. He preferred the wine full strength, a style to which he had grown accustomed while in school in France. After all, he would be having it with food, and only a single glassful. Next, she presented him with a large, dark yellow ceramic plate, with two different edibles on it. At the front of the plate, away from him, were two halves of boiled and cooled baby artichokes—carciofi—lying next to each other, cut side facing down. This wonderful plant, a cultivated thistle with meaty, edible leaves and stem and heart, comes in many varieties and sizes. It is said to have originated in the sands of the Maghreb in North Africa millennia ago, and today is grown in several countries around the Mediterranean, as well as in California and South America. The Italians have managed to cultivate the smallest, most tender and most completely edible of the varieties. Indeed, once boiled in garlic water, and thistle removed from the center, the small ones can be eaten whole, including the leaves in their entirety. Anna poured a few drops of olive oil over them and said with a smile, buon appetito!

The other half of the plate, closest to him, had a large, wedge-shaped piece of something about an inch thick lying on it. It seemed not to be hot, rather, slightly warm and cooling toward room temperature. The color on top was a sort of tan, differentiated with patches of a darker brown, as though the top had been cooked with its surface down on a hot pan before it had been turned over, or it had been broiled by a flame from above it. Interesting as it was to look at, more remarkable were the complex aromas escaping from it: garlic and other herbs, black pepper and spices, cooked egg, warm olive oil, some green but as yet unidentified vegetable, and the compelling odor of a melted, aged cheese, like a rich, sweet, warm butter smell, so good, that it made his taste buds start to quiver. What is this thing? Oh, it's the La Frittata that Anna has been talking about.

He sat for a minute looking at the beautiful wedge, and gently probed it with the side of his fork. It was dense and substantial, but not hard. His fork cut it easily. As he looked inside it, he could see small pieces of cooked garlic, specks of ground black pepper, and melted cheese mixed in with the cooked egg. At the bottom were thin slices of zucchini with their white meat and green skin, that apparently had been laid into the egg mix in the pan before it was cooked. Now that the dish was done, they were fixed in place. What a wonderful piece of culinary architecture, he thought to himself. Forgetting about the artichokes for the moment, he lifted a bite of the frittata to his nose, was captivated by what he smelled, and put it into his mouth. What a revelation! He had never tasted anything like it, nothing quite as good. It was a perfect blend of ingredients, a taste that would please anybody, working man or king. He continued until he had eaten about half the wedge. Then he took a sip of the dry, cool white wine to clear his palate. Now he wanted to taste the jewels on the other side of the plate, the baby artichokes.

As Anna happened to be passing by his table, he hailed her and asked, "Posso mangiare tutto intero?" pointing at the artichokes. She answered back in Italian; Yes, you can eat the whole things. They were almost too beautiful to eat, like two dark green flowers, lying face down on the plate, with drops of olive oil on their leaves, like dew in the morning. But he cut one of the pieces in half, and without remorse, consumed it. What a delightful contrast and companion to the frittata! The green vegetable and the bird protein. The artichoke was sweet and a little nutty, tender enough practically to melt in his mouth, with the subtle flavors of the garlic water it had been cooked in and olive oil working together.

He finished the frittata, the artichoke, the bread, the wine. The experience was almost distracting, as he knew he had eaten something magnificent, something he would like to know more about. He wanted to see the mystique of this dish, La Frittata, revealed. He would ask the women about it. He wanted to make it at home for his parents when he returned to the USA. But he knew if it were in his personal cache of recipes for how to prepare fine food, he might make it anywhere in his travels, given the opportunity. The question became, how to ask Mamma or her daughters for a recipe of some special meal that they prepared with great pride, and that may contain ingredients or techniques unique to their family. As well as the problem of exactly who he should approach.

By late in the afternoons, after five o'clock or so, Mamma was fairly well done with her work for the day. The pensione did not serve evening meals, except on special occasions. Most of the students went out in the evening after studying for a couple of hours and ate in restaurants or taverns. Some kept bread, cheese, and wine in their rooms for a light evening snack. Mamma's habit after her daily duties was to sit at her favorite table in the interior dining room, a large round table next to a windowed door that opened onto a small balcony overlooking the ancient cobblestoned street, where Romans and Etruscans before them had trod. She liked to sit with the door opened beside her. Sometimes her daughters joined her, sometimes not. But there she could be found, along with a demi-carafe of her favorite local red wine, and a small clear drinking glass, and some bread and olive oil. She liked the taste of the local vino rosso, and each week a local farmer friend brought her two five-liter jugs of it. But it seemed to be an acquired taste. The American found it a bit rustic and tannic for his taste. Apparently, others also found that to be true of her choice of table wine. She was generous with the wine if one were sitting and talking with her, and often did not understand why her chat guest was happy with only one glass of it. Fortunately for her residents, it was not the same wine she served at table with meals.

He decided to approach her that late afternoon, at her perch by the opened balcony door. He liked her, and they got along well. She was energetic and easy-going, but had worked hard all her life, and showed it in the late afternoon. Her sense of humor reminded him of his own mother's, a bit slap-sticky, ready to laugh at the silliness of life. He did well with that, as he was accustomed to it from home. On the rare occasion when a disagreeable person crossed her path, she was not one to back down, and loved to call them a buffone, which means the same in Italian as in English. He liked that about her, that she would not back down, and used the buffone word when necessary. She could be demonstrative with her gestures and utterances, like a character in a Fellini movie. Her hands would fly while talking, adding a whole new vocabulary to the conversation. Her facial expressions could change in a nanosecond, from Commedia del'Arte to Tragedia. It was fun to talk with her.

He approached her table, looking her in the eyes, with "Signora, scusa . . . " and she gestured for him to sit down. He asked if he was bothering her, if she wanted to be alone, and she replied in the negative, as she reached for her demi-carafe and poured wine into his glass. She called out for Anna to bring her another demi-carafe, please. He started by telling her how wonderful her frittata was, how extraordinary were the flavors, how beautiful it looked on the yellow plate, and how he had never before tasted anything like it, anywhere. He was ebullient in his praise of her cooking abilities, as everything he had tasted coming out of her kitchen before the frittata experience had also been wonderful, marvelous. He had read Professor

Jacob Burckhardt's two-volume treatise called "The Civilization of Italy during the Renaissance", so he knew how important it would be to praise her culinary magic extravagantly. She seemed almost nonplussed, and at last expressed her appreciation for his compliments. He then proceeded to ask her the big question.

"Signora . . . Mamma, it would be a great pleasure for me, and indeed, a true honor for me, to actually see how you make this magnificent dish, La Frittata, in your kitchen. I am not a chef and make no pretensions to be a chef. But this dish of yours, I would like to be able to make it for my parents when I return to my home in the USA one day. I understand that it is your recipe, and that it may be a private family matter. So I will understand if you decline my request."

She looked at him as he spoke, as if to be reading his eyes. Then she looked out the patio door and studied the scene below. At last, she turned to him and said, "I learned from my Mamma, and she learned from her Mamma, and so on back into the history of our family. And it is a family recipe, but it is not private, as I serve it every week or so, to many people. So you can come to my kitchen and watch the three of us as we make it, so long as you stay out of our way. You are big and will take up a lot of space. But it will be fun to have a man in our kitchen who is interested enough in our food to watch how we make it."

He had been leaning forward on his chair during most of the conversation. When she agreed to his proposal, he leaned back in his chair, smiled at her, thanked her, and gave out a little sigh. She smiled back. They would make their arrangements for his visit to her kitchen.

There was a problem with scheduling. Mamma and her daughters started in the kitchen at about five in the morning every day except Sunday. Their first task was to make the breads and pastries for the day, as these took the most time. A little before eight o'clock they started getting ready for the breakfast meal by making coffee and cutting up fruit, to serve along with the bread and pastries; tables had to be set for service. The students were up and dressed, fed and out the door shortly before nine in the morning. Only after they were gone could a frittata be prepared, which took an hour to make and cook, and a couple of hours to cool, in time for the midday meal. But on important holidays, religious or national, there might not be classes. One of these days was coming up, April 25th, the Day of Liberation—Liberazione! That was the day in 1943 when the Italian Partisans, along with Allied troops, liberated Italy from the German armed forces during World War II.

Mamma invited the American to meet them in the kitchen around eight o'clock on the morning of the Day of Liberation. Although it would be a holiday and no classes, several of the students would be hanging around the pensione, catching up on their studies for the following day's classes. That time of the morning would be a good time, as the rich-tasting Italian roast coffee would be freshest, and much of the early morning's hard work would be finished. Once the students had eaten, the women would start on the frittata.

On the appointed morning, he realized he did not know the way to the kitchen. He assumed it was near the interior dining room, but it was not. Emma found him and told him to follow her. She led him in the opposite direction from where he had been going. They passed through a narrow hall with a low ceiling, all old stone surfaces, then down an old, curved stone stairway of only a few steps. The flight of stairs seemed short, as though the bottom stair put them on a level between storeys of the building. They were deep in the belly of the ancient building that had been annexed to the city wall, and partly excavated into the city wall, facing in toward the town. As they came out of the curve they were suddenly in an open room with high ceilings and long windows to the outside on one wall. Before them was a large room with kitchen equipment and utensils in it, various knives, bowls made of glass or wood, two long wood tables that had seen years of use. At the far end of the long room was a large built-in domed brick oven with a fire chamber under it to hold wood for burning. It was an old affair, still in use, with a narrow chimney vent also made of bricks, that went up the side of the wall and appeared to be vented to the outside somewhere. The tables were festooned with fresh local vegetables, fruits, almonds, over-sized bottles of olive oil, fresh eggs, and large rounds of what looked like dry Pecorino cheese from Umbria, and an enormous cut round of dry Parmigiano Reggiano cheese from nearby Emilia Romagna. Next to the cheeses was a meat cleaver, used for hacking through the dense, hard cheese rounds. Closer to them was a line of string stretched high overhead between two walls, and suspended from it were cuts of fresh herbs, drying for later use: oregano, thyme, rosemary, sage, bay leaf, basil, and more. But the prominent feature of the kitchen was built into the wall facing them on the opposite side of the room from the stairway. It had been there for centuries and was still in almost daily use. And it was an architectural masterpiece, rising there before them. It was an enormous kitchen fireplace, built into the wall, and sticking out from the wall, from floor to ceiling. Its external sides were of granite and sandstone. Inside it, the fire well walls and floor were built of local fire brick, as was the hearth. It was worn and smoke-stained from years, centuries, of use but functioned well. The fire well below its chimney was completely open, and high enough for a grown man to stand up inside it, and wide enough for several men to stand in it at the same time. It was almost two yards deep. It had obviously been designed to cook several large items all at the same time. There were spit scars on the sides of the walls, probably from roasting piglet or large cuts of beef. Mounted on each side wall at different heights above the fire pit floor were long, iron swinging bars for suspending copper water pots or soup tureens for cooking. In the fire pit floor was a large, rectangular iron trivet with six long legs, high enough to build a wood fire under it for cooking. In this magnificent structure, this huge fireplace, was where the women would cook the frittata.

During this labor-intensive process there was a division of labor that the women knew from years of making the frittata together. To begin, a fire had to be started in the fireplace. For this they broke up old packing crates they had saved from food deliveries. The wood in them was thin and dry and would fire up easily. Mamma placed the wood precisely, as Emma and Maria handed her the pieces. This was done quickly, and a fire was started. It would need to get hot and burn down to a lower heat, which would take some time. After the fire was started, Emma went to work hacking the cheese wheels to get large pieces that could be fed into a substantial old-style hand-turned cheese grinder, a cast iron affair that had been made in the 19th century. It still worked like the day it had been made. Maria was busy cutting up garlic and zucchini and grinding black peppercorns. Mamma had before her, on one of the wood tables a large bowl of three dozen or so large fresh hens' eggs, which she was breaking into another large bowl. The empty eggshells she set aside in a bowl to dry, and to be crushed later into smaller pieces for use as compost for her small herb garden. Once done with all the eggs, she beat them with a three-pronged stainless steel utility fork that had a long wooden handle. She held it short, near the prongs, for better leverage and speed, as she beat the eggs smooth. A couple of times she stopped beating for a few seconds, once to add some whole-fat milk to the mix, once to add some of Maria's fresh ground pepper, and a very tiny pinch of salt.

As the women worked, they watched the fire. At one point Mamma told Emma to add some more wood to the center, just a little, and then to leave it alone. At an appropriate moment as the fire was burning down, Mamma left the eggs and walked over to the wall, just to the right of the fireplace. Suspended on a hook was a very large, handmade copper skillet, close to two feet in diameter, with outward sloping sides about three inches in height. It had a long, thick hardwood handle, capable of supporting a lot of weight. On opposite sides of the pan itself, near the outside top edge, were two riveted lifting handles also made from copper, for extra help in case of a heavy load. Mamma gently set the old skillet down on top of the trivet, above the now glowing fire that had burned down to a low heat. She asked Emma to bring her the olive oil and poured about a quarter of an inch into the skillet. Maria brought over some of the garlic she had chopped up, and added it to the olive oil, sprinkling it evenly around the pan bottom. The idea was to heat the olive oil and garlic, but not to burn the ingredients. They knew exactly what they were doing.

 When the olive oil was sufficiently warm, that is, when it was rippling on the surface, but not smoking, Mamma slowly poured the beaten eggs, all of them, into the skillet. She moved the pan a little by lifting the handle, so as to distribute the eggs evenly. That done, Emma and Maria quickly added the pieces of sliced zucchini evenly all around the pan, pushing them down through the egg mix to the bottom, where they would cook in the frittata. Now began the waiting process.

 The goal now was to let the frittata cook slowly from the bottom of the pan up through the egg to the top of the mix. The art was in not allowing the bottom of the egg to burn, while everything inside was cooked through. From time to time Mamma used an ordinary spoon to pierce the top of the cooking egg and look down inside, to see if all was going well. After some time, as the liquid egg on top seemed to be starting to solidify, Emma and Maria approached the skillet with a large bowl of the ground cheese mix and started to distribute it evenly around the surface of the slowly cooking egg, until all was covered with cheese. They had made a mix of two parts Parmigiano Reggiano to one part Pecorino, and now they had to watch the cheese cook and melt to a certain point. What happened next was an amazing act of culinary skill and athleticism.

 Each of the three women now took into their hands a long-handled wooden spatula, not as wide as a pizza spatula, but wider than a spatula used in ordinary domestic kitchens for flipping hamburgers or pancakes. The spatula blade was somewhat flexible, and thin at the lifting end. As there was room at the sides of the fireplace for the women to work, they each went about gently lifting the edges of the frittata away from the pan with their spatula, as though to loosen the egg to keep it from sticking to the pan. When this had been done completely around the circumference of the pan, at a sign from Mamma they each pushed their spatulas from three different directions under the frittata toward the center. Then Mamma uttered the words "Uno, due, tre . . . " and at the count of three, in perfect unison they lifted together the entire frittata up and out of the pan, and in one continuous motion flipped it into the air and over, to land perfectly back into the center of the pan! Not a bit of imprecision, not a speck of food or oil anywhere on the floor or edges of the pan. The frittata was now to cook for the final few minutes on what had been the top side. This process would give it the mottled tan and brown coloring when served at table, because the last act would be when the women removed the skillet from the fire and set it on one of the wood tables. There they would repeat this coordinated act of skill, but this time as they flipped the frittata back to right-side up, it would land on a large ceramic platter adjacent to the skillet, where it would cool for two hours. Then it would be the center piece of another fine midday meal in Perugia, Italy.

Through the years since that time, in several continents and in many countries, including in his own kitchen, the American has eaten frittata, prepared under the best of circumstances by some fine chefs. But he has never since that time eaten frittata prepared and cooked in the same way, in the way Mamma and Maria and Emma cooked it. Maybe other chefs don't know how to flip it, without breaking it. Or maybe they don't have the requisite courage, because after all, if it breaks apart during that process, the dish is wasted, and a complete restart is required. Then how do chefs finish the dish, to give it a golden and mottled tan and brown look on the topside of the dish? Some bake the dish, the lazy chef's technique. Some fire it close up under a broiler, after having cooked it on top of the stove. Broiling it will melt the cheese and finish the dish, giving it a nice look. Some try turning the dish in the skillet, little by little, over onto itself, until it is finally fully turned over, in the meantime dislodging any vegetables that may have been sliced and added to it. But probably no chef does it the way the women did it, by flipping the whole, huge thing with such grace and skill and precision that it lands perfectly, and finishes cooking perfectly. Perhaps that is why it remains the best La Frittata the American has ever tasted.

MONTREAL REVISITED

It was very late in the night. No, it was very early in the morning. It was the last hour of the night before dawn. And it was in the dead of winter.

It was the last hour of night before dawn that the ancient Scandinavians called the hour of the wolf. The last hour of the night, just before dawn, when the most people were born, and the most people died.

It was bitterly cold outside in the dark night. This was, after all, Montreal. Not so far from Hudson's Bay, a very cold place, you know. The vast, cold country of Canada in the winter, covered with frozen snow, everywhere white on white. And the dark, freezing winter nights of Eastern Canada, where the forests are so dense that even in winter when there are no leaves on the deciduous trees mixed in with the pine and birch, the Europeans who came here could not see beyond the first line of trees. But the native Americans, the tribespeople who lived in these vast parts, they could see beyond the tree line, and into the mysteries of the forests. The impenetrable dark to the Europeans was a magical and rich universe to the natives, filled with omens and animals, relatives from the past and sometimes visitors from other tribes, both good and bad. There were even healers, shamans in their ornate dress, somewhere out there in the dark.

The vibrant darkness to the natives was a source of fear to the Europeans. Perhaps this is why it was called Canada by the visitors to this new land, a diminutive or contracted form after the Spanish name Capo de Nada, Cape of Nothing. It was said by the Oldtimers that when the Spanish first sailed to North America in the early 16th century, they sailed into the mouth of the St. Lawrence, the cape near where Quebec City is located today. But, unlike other European explorers who would land and make claims for their respective realms, the Spanish stayed offshore. It was winter, and this new land looked cold, dark, forbidding. The Spanish could see nothing beyond the darkness at the edge of the sea where the land started. They surmised there was nothing beyond where they could see, nothing beyond the hills and forests that ran down to the sea. A cold and bitter and fearsome dark nothing. So they headed south and stayed offshore along the North American continent until they came to warmer climes, leaving behind them the Capo de Nada, Cape of Nothing, Canada.

But now, centuries later, houses and neighborhoods stand where the natives once trod through the dense, dark forests. Montreal had become, since long ago, a distillate of the best features of both the French and English cultures.

The river was nearby, the Saint Lawrence, that huge waterway running north and south through the far eastern edge of Canada. It empties into the Atlantic Ocean in the north by Quebec City. Backing upriver, to the south, it touches the cities of Cap de la Madeleine, Trois-Rivières, Montreal, Cornwall and Massena, Brockville and finally Kingston at the southern end where it meets Lake Ontario. As its water runs downriver, to the north, through the Province of Quebec it picks up more water from tributaries along the way. By the time it empties into the Atlantic by Quebec City, it has become an enormously wide and thunderous rush of water that rivals the power of any of nature's wonders. By Montreal, about half-way on its trip to the sea, the river widens and is more tranquil, moves more slowly, almost silently. It seems peaceful by Montreal.

From the back windows of the house the river could be seen during the day, between the snow-covered pine and maple trees. The view was of a wide part in the river called Lac St. Louis by the locals. They called it a lake, because the water was unusually still and quiet there, or very slow moving, more like in a lake and not like the fast-running water one usually sees in a river.

The hour of the wolf was passing now, and the sky, though still dark, was beginning to show a faint hue of light, as the darkness started to weaken ever so slightly. The closer shore of Lac St. Louis was just beginning to come into view, barely visible, like it was in a dark shadow. This night turning today was very cold and still and quiet outside the house. The house was in one of many small, well to do suburbs of Montreal that lined the lake, places like Ste. Anne de Bellevue, Senneville, L'île Perrot, Baie d'Urfé. This suburb with its large, stately houses and wide yards was a quiet and friendly place to live. The houses were set back from the street far enough that passing cars usually could not be heard from inside unless a window was open. Now in the bitter cold so early in the beginning of morning nothing was moving outside.

Inside the house the tall man, a visitor, was standing by a window at the back of the house, looking out toward Lac St. Louis. He could just see it now, through the trees and down the several yards of sloping open area by its banks. The white of the ground ran up to the edge of the river, frozen lightly there with a white glassy surface covering the water. Other parts of the river were iced over, too. Nothing seemed to be moving near the shore.

He turned to see his old friend, Kassam, approaching fully dressed for the outside except for his parka, and only cloth slippers on his feet. He was walking quietly so as not to wake other members of the family who were sleeping in nearby bedrooms. He spoke softly as he approached the tall man.

"Bon jour, mon ami."

"Bon jour, Kassam."

"Are you ready for coffee?"

"Your coffee, Kassam? Absolutely."

Kassam glanced briefly through a window at the weather outside and gave an expressive shudder, acknowledging the cold. Then the two men turned to walk to another part of the house, the tall man following.

After a few turns through the hallways in the house, an aroma of magical effect could be detected, wafting from the kitchen. It was Kassam's coffee. He used only the best arabica beans, and roasted them himself, to a degree typically called the French roast. Not so dark as espresso, but very dark. Then he would grind the freshly roasted beans into a fine powder, not as fine as espresso, but very fine. He would then brew the coffee by the drip method, not pressing it. He knew just how much hot water to use, how hot the water should be, not so hot as to scald the coffee. And one aspect of Canadian living he appreciated was the water. The tap water in his suburban home near Montreal was fresh and clean tasting. It was good Canadian tap water, perfect for making good coffee.

The tall visitor was not a coffee expert, but he had traveled the world ever since his student days, and knew that chez Kassam the coffee was the best he had ever tasted. Of course, Kassam's French wife made their coffee in the exact same way with the same results. The tall man knew he was in the presence of coffee greatness.

"Alors, mon ami. Here is some sugar and cream for you, mon enfant."

Kassam and his wife took their coffee black. Neither of them could really understand the tall man's heathen habit of adding sugar and cream to a fine cup of coffee. But they tolerated his uncivilized eccentricity. They had known him for many years, and he was their beloved friend. He returned the devotion.

There is a special sensibility that is owned by people from certain cultures toward their food and drink, such as East Indian in the case of Kassam, or French in his wife's case, that is sadly lacking in most North Americans. But their tall North American friend had managed for much of his life to overcome that deficit. The East Indians, the French, and others understand that the multitude of edible flavors and textures in the world are gifts from heaven and earth and should be used to their full extent when preparing food and drink. Hence the richness of their foods and libations. And it was for people from other less expansive cultures to be exposed, at the least, to these riches, so that they, too, could develop their own set of sensibilities. So the visitor felt that it was a blessing for him to be able to experience the exotic culinary delights that sprang from thousands of ancestral years of practice now represented in the Kassam household.

The two men settled themselves in chairs at the breakfast table in an offset corner of the large kitchen to drink their morning coffee. Shortly, they would head outside, and the hot coffee prepared a la Kassam was going to be their last bit of warmth for a while.

The tall man spoke.

"Alors, mon vieux, how are you feeling these days?"

"But for the frigid weather, I feel good, and I feel like I am well. Sometimes I feel great. But it's so cold these past days, I really have to force myself to exercise outside. C'est dur."

"Yes, I know it's hard to do in this weather. We can take a short walk. We don't have to overdo it."

"No, I'm happy to walk, especially along the lake. I'm dressed for it. It's just that once we start, we can't stop 'til we get back here. Or we'll freeze up like a big-rig diesel engine in the Arctic."

Both men had been in the far north in winter. They understood how quickly a truck engine could freeze up and then not re-start in the extreme cold.

"Well, I look forward to the walk. It's been a long time since we last did this."

"Oui. The last time you were here, two winters ago. Even then, it wasn't so cold."

They finished their coffee. Kassam stood up and left the room to find his heavy boots. The tall man was already wearing his and bent over in his chair to finish tying the laces on them. On Kassam's return the tall man rose from his chair and together they made their way through the house to the front vestibule. Well wrapped-up in their boots, flannel-lined pants, parka, scarf and fur hat, the last items were their gloves.

"Ready?" Kassam asked, as he turned the knob on the big oak door, looking back at his friend.

"Let's go," was the reply.

Outside on the front steps of the open porch the cold hit the men in their faces like a cruel weapon of war. The frigid blast took their breath away for a few seconds.

"Jesus!" the tall man uttered. "It's colder than when I arrived yesterday."

"Yes, but it is like this so early in the morning. So we walk a little faster. Cover your face with your gloves until you are a little more used to the cold."

Ice in extreme cold temperatures in the north can, of course, appear to be blue. The slanting, weak rays of the winter sun coming through the earth's atmosphere at a shallow angle to the earth can make the ice appear to be blue, not clear. But on cold days like this in Montreal even the air can appear to be blue, palpably blue, tangibly blue. The air appears even to be brittle, although it is lacking in substance because it is, after all, only air. Nonetheless, the mere appearance of the air as being blue makes one feel even colder.

The men walked at a fair pace up the long driveway to the road that crosses in front of the house. They turned right at the road and proceeded a few hundred yards past other houses and their wide, snow-covered yards to the first corner. A right turn again, and now they were walking toward the lake that was part of the great river.

This suburban neighborhood of wide yards and ample space around each house, and some open, undeveloped lots, was more rural in its feel, almost like a vacation area, where visitors could come to enjoy nature and the out of doors near the water. Now in winter with snow on the road leading down to the lake, one could ski down the road. The challenge would be to get stopped before the snow-covered road turned into icy lake water.

Kassam walked with only a slight limp now, a hangover from his former illness, a sort of paralysis or numbness in his leg. Still not precisely diagnosed, he had stopped taking his medications, felt he didn't need them anymore. His doctor put up a mild objection, but finally acceded to the wishes of his patient.

Besides, Kassam had his own self-designed treatment, completely natural and dietary.

"So, Kassam, how goes the therapy for your leg? You seem to be walking well. We are moving at a good clip."

"Better, since I went off the medication. But my doctor went along with it. He is French, you know."

"Yes, you mentioned that before. And from Provence, no?"

"Oui, which is even better. Actually, it makes him complicit in my treatment. Every time I visit him, he suggests the medication again, I object again. He asks me what treatment I am giving myself, I tell him good red wine, of course. Good for the arteries, good for the heart. He agrees and opens the bottom drawer of his desk. He pulls out a bottle, sometimes a Bordeaux or a Côtes du Rhone, or one of the rich red ones from Provence . . . Then he produces two small aperitif glasses, and we each have a taste of my therapy. It's a very nice arrangement."

"A fine moment for both of you, no doubt."

"But of course, mon ami. He only insists that if red wine is to be my therapy, then it must be a quality wine, a good red wine. This is a medical theory with which I completely agree."

"I like your doctor already, Kassam."

"Yes, of course."

The two men walked on in silence, turning right again when they came to the road that runs along the lake, paralleling the shoreline. The day was starting to fill out with light and texture. But the continuing bitter cold made talking difficult. They concentrated on their walk, looking left at the water and the stillness. Farther in that direction, farther east, the low sun was only a frosted, diffuse, and faint glow of light, barely discernible.

The tall man thought of Provence and the South of France. Ancient, beautiful like few other places, very green, lots of warm sun beside the Mediterranean. He remembered the huge, towering cypress tree outside his bedroom window on the second floor of the house where he stayed with them, and his view of the cultivated hills, the grapevines, the olive trees, the palm trees by the coast. Paradise. The wisdom of that ancient culture, where the inhabitants spend time at their lives, taking the time to enjoy their lives. They relax around food and drink, do the Provencal's. They relax after their meals, too, taking a nap after lunch, or a walk after the evening meal. They relax while preparing the food. To them it is as much about the process, the preparation of the ingredients and the anticipation of how good everything will taste, as it is about the eating of the meal. The tall man thought of the first time he tasted—experienced—Pot au Feu in France. This time it was in the north, in Brittany, chez Kassam. The family was living there for a time, for business reasons. Although his French wife cooked the meal, an art process, it was Kassam who prepared the meats and the vegetables. Everything was laid out on a small wood table before him in a corner of the kitchen. Meticulously and slowly, he peeled and chopped and seasoned or rubbed with herbs everything that would be cooked. Pieces were cut evenly, neatly, precisely. Carrots and leeks and cabbage and potatoes and garlic; pieces of beef and pork and chicken and sausage. The look, the colors, the aroma of the whole mix submerged in a liquid of wine and water and stock, all in a great, deep pot cooking slowly on top of the stove. It went on for hours, even late into the night. It was to be a meal for the next day. As it cooked late into the night, the tall visitor could not sleep, for the aroma drifted into his bedroom, keeping his nose awake. The next day when the meal was served hot that evening, the Pot au Feu was a transcendent experience, as profound an influence on his life in its way as going to school in France or sailing to Africa had been. It was in one way only a fine meal, a table sitting only for a few hours. But the meal released and made present centuries of experiment and refinement by a civilization that has had as a cultural objective the sensuous pleasing of the human tongue and taste buds. "Shall we turn here and head back, mon ami?" Kassam had kept them on the road, where the walking was easier than in the deeper snow off to the sides. The road had been plowed a few days earlier before the last addition of snow to the area. Walking on the road still required some effort to keep one's footing, as the road remained covered with snow, and occasionally ice.

"Sure, Kassam."

It was sufficiently cold, and they had been out there for so long, that each man was now content to withdraw himself back into the warmth of his parka and body coverings. They adjusted their scarves and fur caps and started on their trek back to the house. Feeling the cold getting to their fingertips inside their heavy gloves, they plunged their hands deep into the pockets of their parkas.

The tall man was getting hungry, and assumed Kassam must be feeling the same way. Thoughts of the Pot au Feu stimulated other thoughts of memorable meals chez Kassam. The first time he met them was there in Eastern Canada, many years before. They invited him and some other dinner guests to their home, also on the shores of Lac St. Louis, not far from their present home. He had no idea that during the evening he would experience cuisine extraordinaire. Or that a theory of his about French women and cooking would be reaffirmed.

That evening, long years ago, he had been their special guest. A dining room table had been elegantly set for a dozen invited friends. A twenty-year-old Pauillac was the main wine for dinner, exquisite. But that element, the wine, was only one among several during the evening. Centered on the table was an old French trivet made of pewter, an heirloom from 19th century France. As dinner was served, on the trivet was placed an enameled iron crock pot, still warm from the oven. The crock's iron top was removed, and a complex aroma escaped that expressed every word found in a lexicon of fine cuisine. Although the tall man had enjoyed ratatouille even as far back as his student days in Paris, this was to be a new level in culinary enjoyment. The garlic, the zucchini, the eggplant, the tomatoes, the rest of it had all been prepared by Kassam. Even cutting the snippets of fresh savory leaves free from the stems, not crushing or chopping them, was his job. But it was his French wife who knew precisely how to put it all together and cook it. Surely the Italians, the Greeks, the Lebanese all have their own versions of this dish. But chez Kassam it becomes a delicacy. As Kassam was fond of saying, "If I have the right oil, like from the sunflower or the olive, and the yoke of a fresh egg, and mustard powder, and garlic, and a small pinch of salt, I have all the ingredients to make a mayonnaise. But if I don't combine them correctly, then all I have is a mess."

By that logic when the ingredients of a ratatouille are put together by a culinary artist like Kassam's wife, with just the right wine to stew the vegetables, then the dish becomes high art. Once their tall visitor friend asked her, three days after the dinner event as he was standing in her kitchen eating the last cold remnants of this extraordinary dish, what was her secret? She at first demurred, saying simply that it was just an old family recipe, something they had done in France for many generations. At last she admitted, as though confessing, "It is really the oil, the olive oil. I use the best sweet olive oil I can find. But I do not cook the ingredients in olive oil. There is only a very small bit of olive oil in the pot, when I begin. Just enough to keep the vegetables from burning, even though I use a low heat. And the wine steams them slowly. But when it has cooked, slowly, gently, for a time, and I know it is done, then I let it cool for a while without disturbing it, to where it is still warm. And while it is still warm, I add some more olive oil at that point, maybe one-half cup, straight into the pot. I stir it once or twice gently, so the olive oil can be absorbed by all of the vegetables and herbs and garlic. You can smell the aroma of the olive oil, as it gets warmed by the cooked ingredients. That is when it is at its most divine state." No, madam, your wonderful ratatouille reaches its divine peak the moment it first touches my tongue, thought the visitor.

But for years the tall man had carried a theory in his mind, first developed when he was a student in France, reaffirmed over the years in the presence of French women who prepared food for the table. As a young boy he had a grandmother from West Virginia, who made his favorite dish just for him, which was her fried chicken. There was nothing like it in the world, possibly because it was always so fresh. Grandfather's job was to get the chicken from the garden in the back yard, behead it, gut it and de-feather it, ready it for cooking. In grandmother's hands the chicken became a southern-fried delicacy, a special dish of immense importance.

The years went by, and the young man's experience broadened with time and travel. But he noticed that fried chicken was the only kind of chicken he liked in his home country. Roasted chicken, baked chicken, chicken a la king, any of the fancier recipes all seemed to be lacking. Finally, he determined that it was because, for example, in the case of baked chicken, if the dark meet had been cooked through and was hot inside, the breast and lighter meat was overdone and dry. By contrast, if the lighter meat was still juicy and moist inside, then the dark meat was not sufficiently cooked.

Then one evening when he was a student in Paris, now in his later teens, he had been invited to dine at the home of a student friend he had met, a girl his age. He took the Metro to Neuilly and found his way to rue A. Verien. The girl and her mother lived together in a 19th century apartment building, elegant and stylish. The domicile they inhabited was comfortable and spacious, even when compared to some modern monstrosities found in North America. The main course for the meal that evening was baked chicken, and haricots verts, with accompanying side dishes. This would be his first dining experience to include chicken baked by a French woman, the mother of his friend. But the expectation was the same: if the thighs are done inside, then the breasts will be dry. Why couldn't it be fried chicken?

PART VI

The mother sliced and carved the finished chicken as she had done a thousand times in the past. Like a craftsman who, with his small knife, whittles delicate or decorative objects out of wood. She asked him, would he prefer this piece or that piece? Dark meat or light meat? With no hesitation he indicated this one—then that one! Which one would it be, the light or the dark? Before anyone could get embarrassed, the daughter said, "Tous les deux, Maman!" So the mother gave him one of each kind. As the morsels made their way from Maman's serving fork to his plate to its proper place in front of him, he could not help but notice: both pieces looked warm and done, yet still they were moist. How could this be? He resisted the temptation to use his fork before their filled wine glasses were lifted for a cheerful toast, "Santé!". As soon as the wine glasses had all touched and the first sip was taken, his moment had come. He tasted each piece of chicken on his plate in sequence, first the light, then the dark, and was astonished to find that they both were cooked perfectly!

For the rest of the evening, he was preoccupied with the question: How was this possible? But he never asked. As a foreigner, and a guest in someone's home for the first time, he had the savoir-faire not to ask such questions. But he would not forget the experience. It would have to suffice that he should express himself effusively about the wonder of Maman's beautifully prepared meal.

Then some years later, after having had several occasions to dine on baked chicken prepared by various French ladies in one home or another, as a guest at one meal or another, he developed a theory. One evening, with this theory stored in his brain somewhere, he was invited to a grand meal for a dozen people at the home of Kassam in French Canada. He was treated for the first time to chicken prepared by Kassam's French wife, and his theory was reaffirmed. Actually, in his mind that evening his theory would attain the status of natural law. His theory had been the following: that French women are born with a predisposition, possibly genetic in nature, such that they know how, instinctively, to bake chicken to perfection. That is, French women are born knowing how to bake chicken so that it is neither overdone nor underdone, none of the parts. That the dark meat comes out of the oven warm and moist inside, and so does the light meat. That the epitome of this, let us say, genetic predisposition, results in chicken like the Poulet Agnes Kassam, the chicken cooked lovingly by Kassam's French wife. That night at dinner the tall man knew that the art of cooking baked chicken had been taken to its sublime limits. Now, many years had passed since that first dinner with the Kassams, and after occasional sojourns and visits in France, in Brittany and in Provence together, the two old friends were trudging through the ice and snow of Montreal, mid-winter. They had both been silent for a while, deep in thought and the effort to keep moving before they froze. As they turned up the driveway toward the house, Kassam spoke.

"En fin. We can soon be warm again."

"Yes, but this has been good exercise for both of us."

"Oui. But you were not always here this morning, mon ami. You were somewhere else with your thoughts, no?"

"Yes, perhaps . . . Yes, in truth. I was actually thinking about what, about how much I have learned from you and the missus, over the years."

"Learned? From us? No. What do you mean?"

"Yes, well, I guess it's too long for me to explain. But let me just say, that most of it has been at the dining table. I guess I mean that when you see me smiling a certain smile at the dining table, you will know that I have just learned something else from you. Do you understand, Kassam?"

"Oui, I understand, mon vieux."

The two men entered the house to get warm again, and to start their respective days. Kassam would spend much of it with his wife, having more coffee, planning their day, shopping, paying bills, calling their children and talking with their grandchildren on the phone, watching the television news, and preparing wonderful meals. The tall man would be picked up in a couple of hours by a chauffeur driven car and conveyed the short distance to a meeting in Montreal. Later he would be driven back to the Kassam home. During these local trips he would have time to reflect.

Several years before this most recent visit by the tall man to the Kassam household, his host had been living in the south of France, in the ancient and breathtaking city of Toulon, on the Mediterranean coast. Toulon, favored by the Greeks for its sheltered natural harbor, perfect for trade and for their navy. One of the oldest and most exotic open-air markets in Europe has been open for business almost every day in Toulon since the Romans ran the place. More recently the market has been called the Cours Lafayette, and with twelve months of relatively mild weather, it is a daily food feast for the eyes, for locals and visitors. Toulon, where the young Napoleon Bonaparte in 1793 sent the soldiers under his command up the sheer cliffs of Mont Faron to catch the English invaders by surprise and eject them, humiliated, from the city and from France.

Then in the latter part of the 20th century Kassam and his wife and their teenage son, itinerant as was their custom, had moved south to Toulon in Provence from Brittany in the north. They loved Provence, its sun, its fine weather, its endless vistas of the Mediterranean. Shortly thereafter Kassam experienced a health crisis that left him partially handicapped for several months, although eventually he would recover his health completely.

Some weeks after his episode, the doctors who had managed his crisis, at little cost to him, thanks to the French national health system, felt that he was doing well enough to turn him over to his regular physician. Kassam went to the in-take interview at the office of his regular doctor, a genteel and refined Frenchman, a decade or so younger than his patient. Although the doctor had visited him while he was in hospital, this would be the first time since the crisis that he would resume care for this patient who had seemed so healthy only a few weeks before. So an inventory of Kassam's mental and physical state of being was in order at this point.

The two men were sitting in the doctor's office facing each other from their respective chairs, no desk in between them. After some pleasantries in the style of their local culture, and then some pointed medical questions, including about food intake, the doctor continued.

"Now, Monsieur Kassam, I must ask you some final questions."

"Please, go on."

"Alors, Monsieur, do you at this time drink any alcohol?"

Kassam's mind went into high-speed, seeking the correct answer. He did not know if this were a trap, or an innocent information-seeking question. To ask Kassam, bon vivant and knowledgeable regular consumer of wines since his youth as a student in Paris and Brussels, such a question was possibly to open a Pandora's box full of surprises and maybe, wrong answers.

Kassam retreated to a safe, he hoped, position. He would play his cards close to his vest.

"Oh, a little, I suppose."

Without changing the expression on his physician's poker face, the doctor responded.

"Ah. And what do you drink, that is, when you drink?"

"Oh, it is usually a little wine. With food, of course. As a digestive."

"Of course. And may I ask, what do you prefer, Monsieur? That is, red wine or white wine?"

"Oh, I like a little taste of a nice red wine most of all."

His meekness could have won him the Palme d'Or for acting.

"Ah. Good! A nice red wine. Good!"

Good? Good? thought Kassam. The doctor is on my side! This sounds like it might work out well.

"Yes. Because red wine seems to be most agreeable to me."

"Yes. And may I ask, from which region?"

Which region? thought Kassam. By saying region, this doctor is assuming that I am drinking the wines of France—a good assumption. Otherwise, he would have asked me from which country? From France, or Italy, or California, Chile, Argentina, where? But he asked me which region. Good!

"Oh, well, here in France we are blessed with several regions, no? We have Bordeaux, and the nice Pauillacs that come from there. But not to forget the Rhone Valley. And of course, Bourgogne, and then the wonderful fresh wines of Provence!"

The doctor looked pleased, a smile was coming to his face, and a dreamy look in his eyes.

"Yes, you are absolutely correct, Monsieur! The great wines are here in France!"

Now for the pop quiz. The doctor had one last question, maybe a trick question.

"And may I ask, Monsieur, how much red wine do you drink?"

The synapses in Kassam's brain flashed quickly. In a millisecond, he reasoned: He did not ask me how much per month, or per day, or per meal.

I will show my cards and see if he accepts my hand.

"Oh, one glass, maybe two."

The doctor turned away toward his notes and began to write. He could pursue this further or accept Kassam's answer as is. Per month, per day, per meal? He could let it stand unanswered, let Kassam have his dignity and his red wine. Or—horrors—he could tell him the worst: no more wine!

He turned back toward his patient.

"Ah. Then fine. It is good for you, a little red wine. I have only one suggestion for you, as your doctor of course, Monsieur."

This could be it, this could be where he takes away my wine, thought Kassam. This could be where he tells me, only two glasses per day, or even, per week!

Would this doctor curtail his patient's lifelong pleasure of imbibing the grape? Limit his passion for good wine?

"That is?"

"That is, Monsieur, which ever red wine you choose, I hope it is a good red wine, a quality wine!"

"Ah, but of course, mon Docteur!"

The gates to heaven were now open. The two men smiled at each other, they agreed on Kassam's course of therapy. Then the doctor stood up and walked over to his medical refrigerator. Oh no, thought Kassam, not more medication! I hate medication. I want the natural cures with herbs and vegetables and clean meat that is free from chemicals. And I want my red wine, of course.

The doctor retrieved something from the refrigerator, closed its door, turned, and went back to his chair opposite Kassam. There he presented two small sherry glasses and a chilled bottle of Crème de Mure, an elegant blackberry liqueur, produced in the Dijon area in the eastern part of France. It was a perfect conclusion to their little chat.

The doctor poured the beautiful blackberry-colored liquid into each glass and handed one to Kassam. They lifted their glasses.

"Santé, Monsieur."

"Santé, Docteur, et merci."

"A little of nature's therapy is good for both of us, don't you think, Monsieur?"

"Indeed."

"So, I'm afraid I must leave you now, Monsieur. I have other patients to whom I must attend. But not all with such pleasant consequences."

As the two men got up from their chairs and offered their hands to each other, each had a knowing smile on his face. The doctor opened the door for his patient. As Kassam passed him to enter the corridor, the doctor reminded him.

"Remember, Monsieur Kassam, only good red wine."

"D'accord, Docteur. Of course. Adieu et merci."

"Adieu, et merci à vous."

During his short walk down the corridor to the waiting area to meet his wife, Kassam thought of the many blessings of his life. Even a short list of them was numerous: his wonderful wife; his children; being able to live in several countries, on both sides of the Atlantic, and having friends in each place; the pleasures of good food and wine, along with the good conversation that usually accompanied them; a good life. But today was special. Today he thought the angels spoke to him, through the voice of his doctor.

He saw his wife and smiled at her.

"So, what did he tell you?"

"Oh, he said my diet is good, my therapy at home is good."

"No restrictions?"

"None, except for salt."

"Nothing more?"

"No, nothing more."

His wife smiled, as she could imagine how the conversation must have gone. She had always liked this doctor, and his refined nature made her think he must be one who knows, and enjoys, good wine.

Kassam put his arm around her as they approached the door to leave the clinic.

"I think my therapy is going to work well."

It would do so, and now, a few years later, they would find themselves back in Canada. This was a place where they had lived before Brittany, before Provence, and now they had returned to live in a city they loved, Montreal.

MY HOLIEST DAY

It seems fair to say that there are several thousand uniquely practiced religions around the world, serving a large number of the eight billion (that's 8,000,000,000) of us, we who inhabit the earth as human beings. There is also a multitude of holy days and nights honored by those who practice the various religions around the world.

I am not a religious person, but I am very spiritual. My spirituality is wrapped up in human beings—their art, the edifices they build and decorate, the music and poetry they write, the good they do for the less fortunate among us, the magnificence of the many things they create, the good things they do.

My Dad was an educated man, a Roman Catholic; Mom was an Episcopalian. At an early age Dad was taking me to Sunday Mass with him. In third grade I went to Bible school for a few months at the local Catholic church. But I didn't like it, nor did I like going to church. Finally, when I was ten years old, I told Dad that I didn't want to go to church with him anymore. He was surprised and asked me why. I told him I didn't believe in the Immaculate Conception, nor in the Holy Trinity. He could have argued the points with me, or tried to convince me of the liturgy, but he didn't, he was too smart for that. Instead, he said:

"OK. Here's what I want you to do. If you you're going to be in this house with the rest of us, and we want you here, then each week you have to spend one hour per week with God, that is, learning about God. That means you can go to any house of worship, any church, synagogue, or wherever once a week to learn about God the way other folks do. You can go with your Jewish buddies on Saturday, or the Seventh Day Adventists on Friday evening, wherever you want. But you need to learn about God, and by the time you're an adult, you will decide for yourself how you want to follow a religion. Or not."

Looking back at what Dad did for me that day, I realize how wise he was, and on many occasions. What a great education he just then opened up for me, and I appreciate it to this day. I tried to learn about all of the religions in Dayton, Ohio.

During the first couple of weeks when I was getting to know Linda in 1968, I was appreciating the wide range of topics we could cover in our conversations. But more impressive to me was her crowded and busy life, and her great attitude. Here was a young woman my age who grew up in bad circumstances with no familial support, but rather adoptive family abuse in foster homes. A few years later on, her lousy father, at the insistence of her stepmother, had sent Linda off on a one-way bus trip from Denver to Los Angeles with only fifty dollars in her pocket. She was only nineteen years old. By the time I met her, to support herself she was working two part-time jobs distant from each other, plus teaching guitar, plus going to UCLA to earn a BFA degree, and she never complained about anything. She quickly earned my respect and admiration and would always have it.

As winter turned to spring and summer Linda moved to an apartment in the Ocean Park district of Santa Monica, a couple of blocks from the beach. I soon followed and moved into an apartment next door to her. We were spending a lot of time together, and when she had a break from school or filming, Linda liked to suggest that we drive up to Topanga Canyon for a picnic. The weather was always fine, so we would go shopping in one of the local health food stores for some good quality cheese, nuts, fruit and something to drink, and head for the canyon. Up Pacific Coast Highway to Topanga Canyon Road, and up high into the canyon to the Old Topanga Canyon Road turnoff. By that old road somewhere we would find a clearing of grass alongside it and put our picnic blanket down on the grass and eat and talk. If we had time, we would break camp, descend from the canyon, and drive a couple of miles farther up PCH to the old Serra Road, and follow it up to where it crosses the Malibu Creek. After driving across the shallow water in the creek we would park and go down to the creek to harvest the big round nasturtium leaves from the flowering plants. Then get some rose hips and fennel seeds, all of it growing wild, and head home. Back at one of our apartments we would make a salad with the nasturtium leaves, and Linda would make a tea with rose hips and fennel seeds. These were all sweet times in our Carmina Burana youth.

Between the time Linda arrived in LA and the time we met, about five years, she had worked part-time as a clothes model, done some TV work on *The*

Monkees show, likewise on the *Ozzie and Harriet* show, done a short part in the *Mary Poppins* movie, and had done two USO visits as a singer/dancer with the USO for our Armed Forces in Vietnam, Thailand, South Korea, and Japan. She had also worked as the Space Girl, a prominent entertainment figure at Disneyland. She had also published her first poem at age nineteen.

While at UCLA Linda and I both were involved in campus and national politics and demonstrations, particularly as pertained to anti-Vietnam War, American Civil Rights, and women's rights, the Women's Liberation movement. We were of like mind about all of these issues, as two good young liberals would be in those times.

When I first started at UCLA in the Winter Quarter of early 1969, we were still living close to each other on Third Street in the Ocean Park district of Santa Monica, a couple of blocks from the beach, and very close to the Venice border, as I may have mentioned earlier. One day in very early spring Linda and I were walking down Third Street, between Ocean Park Boulevard on the north, and Rose Avenue in Venice on the south, a three-block stretch. Linda stopped and turned to look up and down both sides of Third Street. Then she said to me:

"Frank, look up and down the street at the grassy strips between the sidewalk and the curb. What do you see?"

I did, and I said: "Nothing but grass on them."

"Exactly. Every other street around here has trees on the grassy strip. Only Third Street does not. That's ridiculous. We need trees!"

"Right! I'm gonna find out what the hell this is all about."

The next morning, I found my way to the Santa Monica City Department of Building and Safety. I approached the counter and told the city employee why I was there. His response was, "Hmmm . . . " then, "Give me a minute, please." And he disappeared. After a few minutes he returned carrying a large, heavy book.

"So, let's see. Third Street, Ocean Park. OK, yep, I see where you're talking about," he said as he turned the pages and landed on one. He studied the page for a few minutes, then looked up at me.

"So, this afternoon I'll go take a look at those three blocks you're talking about. If you've got a phone number, I'll give you a call tomorrow. I need to do some research first."

"OK, cool," I said. I gave him my phone number; we shook hands, and I was off.

That evening when Linda got home from UCLA I told her the story of my visit to the Santa Monica office, and that the city employee seemed to be on our side.

"Whoopee," she said, as she ran up, put her arms around me, and started kissing my face. "Frankie, my hero! You did it again, solved the problem!"

"Nope" I said. "Not me, Linda. It's we, we solved the problem together. Well, it's not yet quite solved. But by the way, you can keep on kissing me anyway." Over the years to come, when she gave me credit for creating forward momentum for some task we took on, I would often have to remind her that it was not "me" but "we" who did it together. It was her generous nature that was so ready to give me credit for things we did together.

She always wanted to give me credit for getting things done, things that she may have thought of doing first, her idea.

A couple of days later the Santa Monica city clerk called me and asked me if I could come to his office. I gladly went. When I arrived at his counter, he pulled out from his papers a large format sheet of lined paper, with a set of matrix columns on it. Inscribed in the left-hand column were the names of six different kinds of trees.

"So Frank, these are the six different kinds of trees that we can plant in the green grass parkway between the sidewalk and curb on Third Street. They are given as choices according to how high they will grow at maturity so as not to interfere with utility lines overhead. Plus, how deep the roots will grow, so as not to interfere with local water drainage or break drainpipes. Also, they cannot grow seasonal berries that will drop on the ground and stain the street or sidewalk and create an unsightly mess."

After looking at the choices, I asked him:

"Can I have a copy of this list to take home, and get back to you tomorrow?"

"Sure" he said.

Back at Linda's that evening I showed her the list and repeated what the clerk had told me about tree limitations. Linda took a quick look and said:

"Bottle Brush! Tell him we want Bottle Brush trees, OK?"

"OK."

The next day I delivered the message of our choice of trees for Third Street, where we lived. Two weeks later, as we came home from UCLA together late in the day, when we turned the corner from Ocean Park Boulevard onto Third Street, new young Bottle Brush trees had been planted on the first block of Third Street and started on the second block. Within three days on all three blocks the new young trees were planted in the grassy strips between the sidewalk and the curb. Today, well over fifty years later, the trees are still there. The neighbors can thank Linda Albertano—poet, performance artist, musician, filmmaker, great human being.

Linda and I were always thinking up ideas to give us an edge toward making extra money. The first year we knew each other we decided to make handcrafted leather goods—purses, sandals, portfolios—because those types of leather products were much in vogue in the late '60s to early '70s. We bought the tanned leather hides, measured them for the pieces, cut them, handstitched them and sold them wholesale to stores on Hollywood Boulevard, to be sold there at full retail prices. We shook hands and vowed 50/50 each at the beginning of this venture that we would do together, and that vow was never broken for all the deals we did together for over fifty years. We always trusted each other, and we never argued about money. Trust, loyalty, having each other's back, and love were the fundaments of our relationship.

We also did something that none of our college friends were doing because we were excellent students with high GPAs, UCLA was giving us grants and scholarships to study there. That great university was and remains demanding of its students and is why it is rated each year academically at the top of the list among all of the state supported universities in the USA. So Linda and I decided to do something so that we would have something after we graduated from UCLA: we searched in Venice Beach for a house to buy. We had enough money to put down as a deposit on a large old two-storey house with a separate bungalow behind it, about one-hundred feet from Venice Beach and the sand, on Wavecrest Avenue. We figured we could live in it and rent out some of the bedrooms and the back house to fellow students. So we approached the elderly lady who owned it, Mrs. Brown, who seemed to like us, so she sold it to us on the spot. This was early in 1970, several years before Venice was "discovered" by the real estate market. At that time Venice was home to artists of all kinds, intellectuals and writers, students and post-grads getting advanced degrees, and some movie makers. Getting the house was Linda's idea, and I was the agreeable support system. We bought it from the nice elderly lady for $30,000. Almost thirty years later, after we had sold it and the new guy renovated it and the small house behind it, the property sold for close to $2,000,000.

When we bought the property in 1970 the large front house had an enclosed front porch, a magnificent brick and tile fireplace with hearth, a large, joined living room and dining room, a bedroom downstairs and a kitchen and bathroom downstairs, plus three bedrooms, a second kitchen and a second bathroom upstairs. We filled the spaces with roommates. After living with strangers for just a short time, good people they were, I started noticing that Linda was a good negotiator when little proprietary tiffs would arise. She had a gentle understanding analysis of tenant problems, and was approachable, easy to deal with. She was also easy for me to talk with about anything.

Her mind was always on the move with curiosity. As to religion, we were alike in that regard, that is, not religious, but very much in admiration of the spiritual nature of mankind. We both were very much against war, and the Vietnam era made us even more so. Linda had been to the war zones in Vietnam, had seen the destruction to structures and the land, but more importantly and tragically, to the people. As a child living in foster homes unloved, she had been victim to some bizarre generally fundamentalist religious teachings, where the following of scripture could oftentimes overwhelm good sense and ethics. For example, she was not allowed to have playmates, nor friends to visit her in the homes, for fear she might be corrupted or be led astray. She determined through sad experience it was really so she could be made to do more housework chores.

As to her spirituality, Linda's like mine was very humano-centric. She was intensely loyal to her friends and would go at length to help them with a project, or if they needed money. But more than that, she believed in her friends, believed in their potential, and in their future. She also believed in the higher meaning of her friends' art, as in her own art. She believed that many works of art are intended to motivate people to a higher end, to take action, to do better by their fellow humans. She was greatly moved by many works of art.

I understood her sensibility. I remember when I was a nineteen-year-old student just newly arrived in Paris. The just past summer I had been working on a famous oceanographic vessel, the RV Atlantis (Research Vessel) for four months, and had experienced weather on the high seas, including Hurricane Alma, that would test any person's faith in humans and whatever made us. But I survived, and was now in La Belle France, getting ready for a year of study. I was walking toward the great and revered Notre Dame Cathedral. It was a late summer afternoon, and the twin west-facing towers were illuminated by the sun like beacons of hope created by the hands and heart of mankind. As I approached, the great statue of Charlemagne greeted me to my right. The

Cathedral's center portals were open to the public, so I walked in, and for some reason wandered several steps to my left and stopped. Then my head started to lift, up and up, allowing my neck to stretch its own length, and allowing my eyes to follow the inside walls of the tower as far as possible, to the shadows at the top. All sound around me silenced, all movement around me stopped. I was transfixed, stopped, unable to move, and just stared up and up. All I could see, all I could envision, was a man from the 12th century stretching himself from a wooden platform almost 200 feet above the earth in order to place a stone in the wall. As he labored there, I could not move. I was planted in that spot for at least five minutes or more, just watching that man. Then the stone was placed, and he disappeared. It could not have been more real for me. I had heard about past lives. Now I started to wonder—about his—and about mine. It would not be the only time I would have such an experience.

If you ever meet me, dear reader, feel free to ask me about my experience when I was doing academic research early this 21st century in the Secret Archives of the Vatican. Or maybe I will just tell you about it anyway at some point in this writing.

Linda and I were a lot alike in certain ways, but with humans and animals she could feel things faster and deeper than I could. She could recognize suffering quickly, feel it deeply and sympathize with it. Dogs, cats, even monkeys that were aggressive or energetic got calm when she touched them or held them in her lap. Amazing to watch. I do not have that gift.

In 1969, as Linda got more involved in film school at UCLA, she realized that filming could be quite physical, long hours and lifting heavy equipment like handheld cameras, equipment boxes, and so forth. So she decided she might be well served to get more exercise. We had spent time jogging on Venice Beach together the first couple of years we knew each other, but school was time demanding, so we had less time to jog on the beach. So Linda went to the UCLA athletic department and asked if she could join the women's cross-country team. She was surprised to learn that UCLA had no women's cross-country team, although they had one for men. Not to be deterred, she asked if she could start one, and they told her she could do so. She met with the track coach, he was skeptical, because she had no real track experience, but he finally acceded, and helped her. For a year she participated in races, with not a lot of success, but she loved the sport, even though for some time she was the only woman on the team. After a while she had to leave the sport, as the demands of film school and academia were more pressing.

But in 1970 she found a physical conditioning alternative a few yards away from our house that we had just bought. At the end of our block in Venice a man named Joe Gold had taken over a small house and started a gym for weight-lifters in it. One day Linda donned her exercise outfit and walked over to the gym and asked if she could work out with the equipment. The young man behind the desk told her she could and let her work out for free for her first visit. She did, and she liked the idea of building her arm strength to manage the heavy Arriflex camera she would be using to shoot her school project. After some time, she had done enough, and went back to the desk to ask if she could join the gym and intended to pay the fee on the spot. But this time there was a different person at the desk, a man named Ken, a body builder. When she told him she would like to join the gym, he became indignant and told her flatly, "No, we don't let women join here.". Linda was surprised, and said she had been allowed to work out, and nobody had objected, nor had anyone told her about the "No women allowed" rule. Apparently, Ken was short on refinement, raised his voice, and got emphatic. Linda started to get emotionally upset. In the meantime, close by lifting weights was a young man who was making a name for himself in the body building world: Arnold Schwarzenegger. He had overheard the entire transaction and sympathized with Linda's request. He was as straightforward with his language as Ken had been rude: "Aw, Ken, don't be a jerk! She's not hurting anything, let her join the gym! We should let women in here, they want to work out, too!" Words ensued, Ken tried to claim that Joe didn't want women in the gym, Arnold denied that claim. Finally, Linda was able to pay the fee and join the gym. Joe the owner never had a problem with it. Linda became the first woman to join Gold's Gym, so far as we know. She had struck a blow for women's rights, with the help of a man! Linda would be a member of Gold's Gym for the rest of her life.

In the aftermath of the episode with Ken at Gold's gym, a couple of weeks later Linda invited Arnold over to a thank-you dinner at our house. It would be in our charming upstairs kitchen and dining area, and the menu would include a body builder's favorite food items: huge prime steaks. I would not be able to attend, as I was busy, but I met Arnold, exchanged pleasantries, and went on about my business.

Linda and I both graduated from UCLA in the very early '70s. We both were Honors graduates. Linda was awarded First Prize for her student film, a real accomplishment against about fifty other films, which led to her being hired by Anne Bancroft's production company. Linda went on to make three films with Ms. Bancroft before she took a break from filmmaking. I graduated Summa Cum Laude in Philosophy and European languages, and was elected to Phi Beta Kappa, which led to a research and teaching Fellowship in the Philosophy Department. For various reasons each of our career paths changed within the next couple of years. Linda did not particularly like working in the technical end of filmmaking, rather seeing herself as an auteur filmmaker, in charge and taking the risks, doing the writing, and directing. I had the sad experience of losing the professor I wanted to work with on my Ph.D. dissertation to a tragic accident that took his relatively young life. I had great rapport with him, and the lethal event caused me to rethink my trajectory.

So we both did what any well-educated, well-travelled couple would do for a change of pace: we both went into the restaurant business, in LA! OMG! In any event, over the next four years Linda became the first female head manager of a very successful quality dinner house in a chain called Victoria Station. I became the head manager, with an ownership plan, in a Canadian chain of large format Italian restaurants called the Noodle Factory. With the money I made there I went into the used classic airplane business with my great friend James Turrell, the famous American artist. We both had and still have commercial pilot's licenses. After a while I transitioned out of the restaurant business, and between flying and working as an independent contracting consultant for the U.S. Small Business Administration, I did well. Linda decided to leave Victoria Station and opened her own Italian restaurant, and after a couple of years sold it well. All the time, she was writing poetry.

But in 1980 Linda and I formed our own company, the LA Marketing Group (as in Lutz Albertano Marketing Group). We had always been interested in good nutrition and healthy nutritional supplements. We had decided in the first year we knew each other to take nutrition supplements, plus no smoking (neither of us had ever smoked), no drugs, no drinking of hard alcohol, and to follow healthy habits, like exercise, which I had always done as an athlete; she had done as a healthy habit. She also loved to dance, and for several years we went together to folk dancing venues in LA. It gave her great joy.

We formed and worked our LA Marketing Group and worked together in it for forty-three years, until she passed away. We became independent contractors with the huge worldwide nutrition and weight control company based in LA called Herbalife International. We would do well by that great company and went on to become among its first Hall of Fame members. During the 1980s as our own company grew, it generated enough income for us to spend time following our other pursuits: Linda with performance art and poetry, and me with more academic involvement at UCLA, in the Center for Medieval and Renaissance Studies, where I still am a Council member. The Center sponsored me to do academic research at the Vatican Secret Archives in Rome; I still have a Vatican pass.

The '80s and '90s were prolific decades for Linda's endeavors in poetry and performance art. Her poetry presentations and performance art pieces had been gaining attention in the art world since the late '70s in many small venues and private spaces. Beyond Baroque in Venice had welcomed her early on, and she became a fixture there, a place she loved. In the '80s she was a regular at the Lhasa Club in Beverly Hills. But then larger public venues were looming. The City of Santa Monica commissioned her to do a remarkable multi-cultural performance piece about the history of California that she would write, direct, and perform in, called Calisaladia, on Santa Monica Beach. Then there were MTV's *The Cutting Edge*, UCLA's *Schoenberg Hall*, Allen Ginsburg's *Memorial AMERICA* at the Wadsworth Theatre, The John Anson Ford Theatre in LA, New Langton Arts in San Francisco, Sushi Gallery in San Diego, London's October Gallery, Edinburgh's Edge Theatre, the One World Poetry Festival in Amsterdam, and the Getty Museum in LA. The list goes on to over one hundred major venues in North America and Europe.

In 1986, Linda was commissioned to write, produce, and present the first performance piece, a multi-cultural play, in the newly remodeled LA Theatre Center in Downtown LA, a prominent theatre space. The piece was called "Joan of Compton"—Joan of Arcadia, and featured a cast of poets, artists and a 30-member marching band that Linda had discovered in South Central LA. With two wonderful friends, Laural Ann Bogen and Suzanne Lummis, Linda formed the troika they called the Nearly Fatal Women, whose mission it was to save the world through poetry, which they did well. The trio travelled the USA and Canada to present versions of their award-winning poetry. Twice during the '80s Alice

Cooper asked Linda to join his company for world tours with his Nightmare and Nightmare Returns stage shows that would visit venues in the USA, Canada, and Europe to huge sellout crowds. Linda played the Evil Nurse, and the Executioner. Alice and his company performers later would be awarded Platinum records for these shows. In 1987, for the second tour, the Nightmare Returns show, Linda was actually in a clinic in Mexico, undergoing treatment for breast cancer, which turned out to be successful. I was with her there. Alice Cooper called her there to invite her on to the tour. "Are you in, Linda?" "I'm in—let me tell my doctor!" Her doctor was very OK about this and gave Linda enough medications and syringes for the duration of her trip. He also fitted her with a shunt in her brachial artery high on her chest, so that she could daily self-medicate with the serum he gave her. It all worked fine!

Linda was also very involved in women's issues during these years and had been since we were at UCLA. She used her poetry and her public visibility to advocate for women. In addition to her work with Nearly Fatal Women she appeared with groups like Word Women, LA Woman, and Divas 3.

In 1999, Linda and I spent a summer Sunday at a local festival on the Dorsey High School property in LA. At one point we heard through the crowd and into the distance a beautiful, lilting stringed musical sound that was not familiar to either of us. We followed our ears and came upon a platform raised about three feet above the crowd with a young colorfully dressed African man and an amplifier on it. He was holding a large round globe of some kind, larger than a basketball, that had a long, stringed piece of wood sticking out of it. The wood neck had twenty-two gut strings affixed to it, and it was strung like a harp. He was playing all of the strings with both hands and singing in an African language. We listened with intrigue, and when he took a break, Linda went up to talk with him. He was quite accommodating and told us his name was Prince Diabate from Guinea in West Africa. Having travelled all over Africa, I was familiar with Guinea's location. This first meeting would be the beginning of a long and lovely relationship between Prince Diabate and us, from 1999 until late in 2022, when Linda passed away.

Prince was temporarily visiting friends in LA, and staying with his wife Linda, an English lady, in a house in Venice near us. My Linda determined that she would like to learn how to play the instrument, called a kora (or Kora), and Prince agreed to give her lessons. Linda already played the piano and guitar, so she progressed well on the Cora. She got to the point in a year so that she could back up Prince in the rhythm sections of the West African songs he played. Prince for a while had made Venice his base of operations, and made friends with other West Africans living in LA. He and Linda started doing some gigs together, and later Prince expanded his group. In the early 2000s Prince needed to spend some time with his family in Guinea and invited us to visit him there. Linda could learn more about other West African instruments, including their bass called the Bolon, and their five-stringed guitar called the Ngoni. So off we went to Guinea!

We flew first to Paris and stopped there for a short visit, always a pleasure, Paris. Then it was a six-hour flight south to Conakry, the capital of Guinea. When we landed and departed our Air France plane, Prince had a West African band comprised of his musician buddies waiting to greet us—it was great! There were about ten of them, all playing different African instruments, and dressed in the colorful styles of West Africa. We drove through the town of Conakry, and its French Colonial buildings, out of action traffic lights, and massive open drainage ditches running parallel to the streets and right next to them, that handle the seasonal floods from monsoon rains. We wondered how many cars at night would end up in the ditches, as they were not easy to see.

Our first accommodation on this first trip was in a lovely area of palm trees and flowering shrubbery, set back off the street in an area not far from the center of Conakry, and its main open-air market. The rooms were actually free-standing small, beautifully decorated transport wagons on stilts. For each room to include a bedroom space, and sitting space, and a full bathroom including a shower required two wagons that each has a side removed and then the wagons bolted together from the outside. The ceilings were about nine feet high. The beds in these accommodations all had overhead drop-down mosquito netting. This was, after all, West Africa.

In between Linda's Cora lessons given her by Prince, or lessons in another instrument provided by one of Prince's musician buddies, we had time to visit the town and the countryside where Prince was building an international music school for West African music. While we were there, Prince gave an evening concert with him on the Cora and several other instruments played by his friends, in an open-air space in a nearby forest by a low waterfall land stream. Quite a beautiful experience.

The first trip to Guinea was a big success for Linda, and she continued to work on the Cora at home in Venice. Prince over the years made several trips to LA, and we would return to Guinea again in the '90s. Linda and Prince played duet concerts with the Cora and Bolon around California and the USA, and occasionally concerts with a fuller ensemble including other instruments. We also helped Prince, legally and otherwise, become a proud citizen of the USA.

Over the years people have asked me what was the driving force that made Linda want to become so accomplished in so many areas of the arts, and especially poetry, her favorite art. By her own analysis, Linda's artistic compulsion came right out of her rough childhood. When she at age eight and her brother at age four and her mother were all abandoned by her father, her life became a nightmare. She and her little brother were then separated from Alberta, their mother, and to increase the tragedy, the two kids were put into separate foster homes, not to see each other again for years. While Linda was kept in various foster homes until the age of sixteen, she was treated poorly. For example, she was not allowed to eat with the family, but had to take her meals in her room. She was used by the family as a maid servant and was not allowed to invite friends into the homes. She was not allowed to voice an opinion or an objection. She often had poorly fitted shoes, which caused her pain. And so on. When she was liberated from foster homes at age sixteen, she went to live with her father and a stepmother. That became another form of torture, because her father was passive and dominated by her stepmother, and her stepmother treated her poorly. This despite the fact that Linda was an honor student in high school, likewise in college at University of Colorado, Boulder, and was voted Homecoming Queen her second year there. Finally, her stepmother prevailed over Linda's weak father, and cut Linda off from any financial help for college. She also wanted Linda out of the house. So at age nineteen her father gave her fifty dollars plus a one-way bus ticket to LA, and took her to the bus station to see her off.

When I met Linda in 1968, she had already been in therapy for several years, and would continue in therapy for the first twenty years I knew her. In LA, she started in therapy at the Suicide Prevention Center, a compassionate and free service for people in a severe personal crisis. Linda continued there for several years under the care of a wonderful therapist named Dr. Tim Brown. Linda told me that when Dr. Brown went into private practice, he refused to let her pay for his services, and that was true for many years, until Dr. Brown retired and moved out of state. I contacted Dr. Brown after Linda passed away. Her last letter was to him, thanking him for his help. He expressed to me that he always believed in Linda, and that he only wanted her to succeed. I understood that sentiment.

I know that one of the reasons Linda liked me and that we got along so well was because she could say anything to me, talk about anything, express any opinion, object to something I might have said, and it was all OK. But she liked other people for the same reason, that is, they let her be heard. And so did her poetry let her be heard.

I was awakened by UCLA Hospital, Santa Monica, cancer ward at 4:45am on the morning of Tuesday, September 13, 2022: "Mr. Lutz, I am sorry to inform you that your dear wife Linda has passed away this morning at 4:40am." I had been up for 48 hours prior to that, going between the hospital and home, doing chores, looking after business. I had kissed Linda goodnight on her forehead at about 9:00pm the evening before; she was already asleep, under medication. Now here I was, returning to see her for the last time in this life. It was the worst moment of my life. The week before this, on Tuesday, September 6th in the afternoon we had got married for the second time and in her hospital room. It was the most joyous and happy moment of our lives! We were laughing and crying and kissing and hugging each other. Now I was here to kiss her goodbye. I kissed her on the forehead and sat down beside her, held her hand, and kissed it. While holding her hand I looked at her face and said, "Linda, I will love you forever. And when you see my time is near, I want you to beckon me, like Virgil beckoned Dante, and like Dante followed Virgil, I will follow you. And I will find you again, my Love. And I will love you forever." I kissed her hand one last time, stood up, and walked over to the door. There I turned around and looked at her for several seconds, for the last time . . . until . . . I will see her again.

A few days after she died, I got her laptop computer out of her things I had brought home from the hospital. Her last entry in the computer was on Monday afternoon, September 12th, at 2:20pm, a poem she was working on. Only fourteen hours before she died. She had been projecting new readings, new shows into September, October, November. She was not giving up! She was fighting to the end!

She, that wonderful woman Linda Albertano, was devoted to that ancient art, that ancient craft of poetry, the song of the heart, up until very close to the time she died. Dr. Brown, who knew her longer than I did, helped her along with his expertise and his goodwill, knew she would do something spectacular with her life. He loved his patient, and she loved her doctor, for giving her the chance.

I recall something my dad had said to me. "Frankie, a lot of people think that music is the highest form of art. But I don't. I think that poetry is the highest form of art." I asked, "Why's that, Dad?" He responded, "Because the purpose of poetry is to elevate the language, to make it easier for people to express themselves in beautiful ways, whether it be for their emotions, or their perceptions, or ideas, and so forth."

And the holiest day in my life was the evening I met Linda the poet for the first time, in 1968.

SHE SAID: "I WANT TO BE HEARD . . . !"

So what drove Linda to do her poetry? I asked her that years ago. Her response was emphatically: "I want to be heard!" That was it. Sometimes she said it loudly, or forcefully. Other times she said it softly: "I want to be heard!"

During the '80s and '90s Linda continued to focus mainly on poetry and performance art. She was becoming well known, always well received and well-reviewed. She was consistently very creative and artful with her performance art stage settings, whether in a large outdoor venue like the John Anson Ford Theatre, or a small venue like Beyond Baroque. In addition to public venues, she was asked to present her poetry in private settings and public schools and universities. She presented her poetry in venues in this country and abroad. Her poetry was getting published in many magazines and books, including: LA Institute of Contemporary Arts Journal; Invocation LA; Twelve Shades of Red; Gynomite; Beyond Baroque Press; Tribe LA Magazine; Wide Awake; Maintenant (DADA); Performance Arts Journal; and many others. In 1997, she was asked to write and present a dedicated poem at LA's Wadsworth Theatre at the Memorial for the great Beat poet Allen Ginsberg. She was commissioned by the LA Port Authority to do a series of poems about local coastal port waterways, and the lives of people and animals living and working there; likewise commissioned by the LA RTD to do a series of poems on the lives of people who work on and use the new Blue Line for transportation. She was also in demand for newspaper and magazine interviews. She presented at the October Gallery in London, the One World Festival in Amsterdam, the Edinburgh Festival in Scotland, Lollapalooza in Chicago, and the Southwest Music Festival in Austin. In 1989, she was proclaimed as the best woman performance poet in Los Angeles. Her poetry and performance art during the '80s and '90s had pushed her renown both in the USA and in Europe to the extent that in 2001 she was among six prominent Venice poets whose names and lines of poetry were engraved in the famous Venice

Poets Monument wall on Venice Beach. Like the words of Homer were engraved in stone walls 2,800 years ago in Greece. Linda was also one of the very few lady poets ever to be given the name "Poetry Diva" by the City of Los Angeles.

During the 1980s, Linda and I were assertive about securing our financial future. We had already bought our first home in 1970. A few years later, with a married couple who were good friends, we bought the property next door, held it for a few years more, and then sold it for a decent profit. Now we had some more money for investments. Linda and I had no family money, no backup, just each other. We never once argued about money, the use of it, and we trusted each other implicitly, our honesty and our judgement, for all of our time together. As our nutrition products marketing business began to grow and yield more income during the '80s we started to look around for ways to invest and settled on what we had been taught through our limited experience in real estate and property. During the coming decades we would invest in other states like Arizona, Montana, and Texas. We also invested in residential properties in Costa Rica, Panama, and Nicaragua. Were all of the investment's winners over time? No. But the overall average success rate was definitely in the plus column. Once we started making enough money, we started donating to more causes that we believed in. Linda loved people, and so she had automatic donations taken out of her checking account or credit cards to about twenty charities or funds each month. Because she loved people, she wanted to care for those who needed help.

Something I noticed about Linda the first time I met her was that she was an elegant and colorful dresser, even in cowboy shirts, jeans, and cowboy boots. She was tall, about 6'4", had a great shape, and was very beautiful. She also had a great mind and sweet personality. I am about 6'6" so it was easy for us to look each other in the eyes when talking. As time went on and she bought more clothes—pants, tops, shirts, jackets and so forth—she always picked out great colors. She especially liked shades of black, gold, purple, and red. She avoided browns, yellows, most pastels, and drab colors. Her mother Alberta was also an artist, and a very colorful dresser, but in the primary colors of the spectrum typical of American made garments. Linda was attracted to the more subtle and varied European colors and blends, and looked wonderful in anything she wore. She had a collection of over one hundred multi-colored chiffon scarves from all over the world; obviously she loved chiffon. She credited her mother for giving her a penchant for colors, as in this direct quote: "Any good characteristic I have I got from my mother."

So as we travelled for business, music or poetry, or pleasure in both hemispheres of the globe Linda always had her eyes opened for colorful clothing, and other pieces of raiment, and even local jewelry. Of course, Mexico and the southern reaches of the western hemisphere, and West Africa were all of especial interest to her. She brought home to California costumes made for her in West Africa, which she wore on stage and in other venues where she and Prince Diabate played. It turns out that in the LA Basin there are living here several thousand native African people, many of them from the several countries of West Africa. It was always an expressed thrill for them to see Linda and Prince onstage clothed in their African styles.

During the early part of the present century Linda continued to work on developing her skills as a player of both West Africa musical instruments, the Kora and the Bolon, as she and Prince played venues inside and outside California. The two study trips we had made to Guinea in West Africa had been seminal in her mastering the music. But she was also in demand for her poetry and performance art. She would appear at the LA Sacred Music Festival, the Madrid Theatre performance center, Royce Hall, The Getty Museum, the Queen Mary, the California Plaza, the Aquarium of the Pacific Poetry Cruise, the Angel's Gate, and many other venues. And there were always performances with her two pals, Laurel Ann Bogen and Suzanne Lummis in their poetry and performance art trio The Nearly Fatal Women. Along the way she would also receive more awards of recognition such as from the City of LA as a bona fide Poetry Diva.

So far as we knew, life was good, we were happy, and Linda continued to produce poetry, her first love of the arts, and present it. Her mantra of "I want to be heard!" continued to bear fruit. In 2019 I had started making plans to return to Rome, to the Secret Archives of the Pope in the Vatican, to complete my research for an academic project I had started several years prior. I have been for many years a Council member at the Center for Medieval and Renaissance Studies at our alma mater, UCLA. My project dates back to Pope Nicholas III in the 1280s, and I had answered one of my historical questions in my prior visit to the Vatican. So I wanted to search through the ancient writings to find the answer to my second question, if possible. Of course, I would take Linda with me, as she loved our prior visits to Rome. My Vatican Pass was still good, and they had their dossier on me. At this same time, at Linda's suggestion, we started thinking about publishing a book of our poems together.

Then Covid hit the world. As we all know, international travel was interrupted, and if you could go anywhere, you ran the risk of infection everywhere. So for the following three years we limited our travel to the States and California. Finally, in 2022, the situation seemed to be getting better, the people of the world were more optimistic.

Linda and I both had got the vax, and we both had short bouts with Covid. We continued to lead our healthy lifestyles, as we had been committed to that for decades, both as lifestyles, and as a business. However, Linda did get five different negative reactions, or side effects, to her first vax, and elected not to get any further vaccinations for Covid. Understandable, and I supported her decision. She reported the bad reactions to the medical authorities, but no response from them. Not understandable. But now in early 2022 we were becoming more optimistic about travel.

Then on the morning of Thursday, April 7, 2022, Linda woke up in bed and said to me as I was moving around in the apartment "Hankie, I feel a lump in my tummy. I think we should go to the doctor." I responded, "Absolutely!" Thus began a long journey for us to try to save her life.

In 1987, Linda had been told by her doctor of that time that she had breast cancer. The answer was for her to have a mastectomy. Linda would have none of it, and so we determined to seek out alternative treatment, both in the USA and abroad. We had heard about the Cancer Control Society in LA, so we contacted them; they were a great resource. From Venice we travelled to Lemon Grove, California by San Diego, to the Optimum Health Clinic, AKA: Hippocrates Health. There we would stay for two weeks, living on their organically grown fruits, vegetables, grains, chicken and wheat grass juice. In our spare time we drove across the border into Tijuana and Ensenada, Mexico, to visit the various health and cancer clinics there. The clinic that Linda liked the best was started and run by an American named Jimmy Keller, who had been a cancer victim himself. Jimmy had a proprietary serum that he or a nurse would inject IV into Linda's arm each day. It was a slow drip that would take several hours. During the day we stayed in the clinic, and in the evening, we drove back across the border into San Diego to our motel. It was an easier drive in those days. One day Linda got a call from Alice Cooper inviting her to go with his troupe on their second Nightmare World Tour, the Nightmare Returns. Of course, Linda told Alice: "I'm in!" She was near the end of her two-week stay for treatment, but the

Keller Clinic also prepared some serum for her to take with her on the tour with Alice Cooper. Jimmy Keller had a shunt installed into her upper brachial artery so she could easily give herself an injection of serum each day during several days of her trip, which she did. The treatment was a success, Linda's tour was a success with Alice Cooper, and the entire group a couple of years later received Platinum Records because the music from the tour was a huge success! And Linda would live on, and create her art, for another thirty-five years.

Now we were in 2022.

On April 7, we went into action to investigate Linda's condition. We contacted UCLA Medical to see Linda's doctor in Family Medicine. Then a series of tests were scheduled over the next few weeks. We asked to have the time spans for the tests to be shortened, which for the most part they did. In the meantime, we began researching alternative care in the USA and Canada, and other countries, in case the news we got would be bad, i.e., cancer.

At one point in May 2022, Linda received a call from her dear friend and fellow performance artist, who for privacy reasons will remain unnamed, who lived a twenty-minute drive from us. She was Linda's age, very ill, and asked Linda to come visit her. I drove Linda to the lady's apartment, and waited outside, to give the ladies a chance to speak privately. A short while later Linda returned to my car, and we drove home to Venice. On the way home Linda explained to me that her friend had been undergoing cancer treatment for the past year, which consisted mainly of chemotherapy. The lady explained that she was mainly bedridden, was in constant pain from the cancer and chemotherapy, that she had no life and was terminal, and had decided to end her life with the legal assistance of licensed doctors, which is legal in California if the doctors and the patient all follow the correct legal procedural steps. Linda understood her friend and was supportive. They then said an emotional goodbye, the lady assuring Linda that she would be notified when it happened. A few weeks later, it happened. A few weeks after that, during the summer of 2022, Linda was asked to speak at her friend's Memorial, which she did.

Linda had always maintained that she would never want to go through chemotherapy if she had cancer. She would rather live out her life and enjoy it while she could and be put on pain medication toward the end.

A few weeks after her friend's passing Linda and I headed for Rosarito Beach, Mexico, a suburb of Tijuana. We would spend the first two weeks of June in the world-famous Gerson Health Clinic, so that Linda could undergo their natural and medically assisted protocols for combatting serious health challenges. The Keller Clinic was no longer in Tijuana, as a lot had changed there since 1987. We had known about the Gerson Clinic since our first trips to the Tijuana area, and Linda had said if she ever got seriously ill, she would want to go to the Gerson Clinic. So there we were, in that pleasant place. The clinic compound has accommodations for about twenty-five patients, plus an adult family member with each patient, to live onsite in a nice apartment for the duration of their two weeks stay. It is fully staffed 24/7 with medical doctors, nurses, and nutrition advisors. Many of the doctors have been trained in and practiced in both Mexico and the USA. The meals are served in a main dining room at a large dining table that can accommodate all of the guests at the same time. It is a friendly, calm, and beautiful environment.

In the case of patients with special needs or tests, a specialist doctor can be called in to do a test. In the case of Linda, once we were settled in for a couple of days and some tests were run on her, they called in a specialist for a second opinion as to her condition. A tall, pleasant Mexican medical doctor came to the clinic to examine Linda. He had taught medicine in Mexico and at Princeton University. When he met us and during some small talk, I mentioned that I had been a combat medic NCO in the US Air Force Reserves and had worked in ER. He invited me to help him with the procedure on Linda, which took about one-half hour and was basically a CT scan of her abdomen. I obliged and steadied her body in several positions while he did the procedure. As he worked, he uttered some soft "umms" at various times, and he indicated some places inside her abdomen as shown on the computer monitor. After he finished and we had helped Linda get upright, he mentioned what looked like to him some "aggressive" cancer cells in her lower left abdomen. He said that he would like to do a repeat examination in about ten days, just before we were to return home. After the test and the doctor's comments, Linda did not outwardly seem to react to what he had said. She continued to be friendly, approachable, and gregarious, per her usual public persona. But we both were very concerned. We did not need to verbalize it; we could read each other. We had been very close and loved each other for a long time.

Our stay at the Gerson Clinic, just a short block from the beach, was a lovely time, despite our reason for being there. We met some great people there, both medical folks and patients. We knew when we left to return home, we would probably never see any of them again, for a variety of reasons.

When we returned to Venice in mid-June it was a series of more exams for Linda at UCLA Medical in Santa Monica and Westwood. None of the news was good. She seemed to be holding her own physically at that time. We were doing a multi-faceted protocol at that time, which included cryotherapy, hyperbaric oxygen, infra-red therapy, ultra-sound therapy, and other procedures. In mid-July Linda seemed to be having trouble walking with me on our longer walks around our neighborhood. She also seemed to be tired more often, took little naps, which was not like her. She continued to work in our office, she continued to write poems and plan new shows.

In another short story I have written called "On the Life of Linda J. Albertano" and included in this book I wrote about a conversation Linda, and I had in July when she told me she thought she might die. I was upset with the thought of that and told her I would rather die than to see her die. You can read the entire transaction in that story. Now we were facing that prospect. In early August, her lower abdomen started to get larger, like swollen, and she complained of some pain. We went to UCLA Med in Santa Monica, more tests. They determined that she was starting to get a collection of some bodily fluids called "ascites" in her lower abdomen which was causing the swelling. The ascites fluid was not a part of the urinary system, rather it was fluid created by organs that were affected by cancer and could not be eliminated through the ureter. It would have to be eliminated, drained, from time to time by a long needle injected into the abdomen, a standard procedure.

On Saturday, August 13th, 2022, Linda gave her last public stage presentation of one of her poems at a gathering of LA's most prominent poets in the Los Angeles Main Public Library. She was excited to be one of the invited honorees. She read her poem "Beloved" to a packed auditorium. It was a wonderful event. She was happy she was able to be there. I had to help her walk, as she was unsteady by now. I had to help her walk up the short stairway to the stage, once on the stage another poet helped her to the podium. As she grabbed the podium and began to read, she lit up like a Christmas tree! She was full force with her wonderful voice! After she finished and the crowd applauded her, she needed help again, coming down from the stage.

At home for the rest of August she mainly stayed inside, except for a few assisted walks close by with me on the Ocean Front Walk. Every third day we needed to go to UCLA Med in Santa Monica to drain her abdomen, which was not painful, just inconvenient. So they installed a permanent catheter in her abdomen so that we could drain it at home, which we did.

At one point in August, I came upon her midday taking a nap on her day bed, facing her windows and with a full view of the beach and our beautiful Pacific. I memorialized that magical moment in a poem I wrote called "L'Amour Pour Toujours (Love Forever)," and it is included in the first book I wrote about Linda, entitled *On the Life of Linda J. Albertano*.

As August and its very hot weather wore on in 2022, Linda was eating less and needed her abdomen drained more often. She was active at times, working in our office, or in her easy chair in one of our apartments, typing poems and an occasional email or letter. She always seemed cheerful to me; I believe it was because she loved me so much and did not want to upset me with her predicament, and her sadness. She knew I was 24/7 doing everything I could do to help her. She left me sweet notes.

Just before midnight on Friday, September 2nd, Linda complained of a lot of pain in her lower abdomen. I looked at it, and it seemed swollen more than usual. We had just drained it on Thursday. So I took her to UCLA Med in Santa Monica. The staff knew her by now, and always treated her well. After some tests, they said she needed to be admitted to the hospital so they could keep their eyes on her for a couple of days. I stayed with her for a few hours and kissed her good night at about 4:00am. That night had turned into the day of Saturday, September 3rd, my 80th birthday.

Linda was made comfortable in a room with a view on the cancer ward of the hospital. On Saturday I brought her some belongings and her laptop computer. She would make use of the computer every day until her last day. She continued with her wonderful smile to greet me every time I came to be with her, which was daily. She was having tests done daily, an ascites drainage as necessary. She had stopped eating, as the pressure of food in her stomach combined with the build-up of the liquid ascites from below in her abdomen was painful. She was taking in minimal water and some other liquids. Friends were visiting her when possible or calling her.

As I was taking care of business early in the mornings at home, running errands, and getting to the hospital as soon as I could, I missed out on some of the interaction with friends and hospital staff. On Tuesday morning at 10:30am I was on the phone with our dear friend who is also our accountant, Larry. He was calling to see how Linda was doing. I have detailed this funny and wonderful episode in the story "On the Life of Linda J. Albertano," which I have included in this book. We were talking calmly when suddenly Larry, completely out of character, started yelling at me: "Frank, you two gotta get married." I was dumbfounded as he had been our accountant for forty-seven years and knew that we had done a California Domestic Partnership about twenty years earlier. But Larry sensed something else. He said: "No, I mean a real marriage!" I was quiet, as I tried to process it all, and I agreed in my mind, it would make both Linda and me deliriously happy to just do that.

Later that day I arrived at Linda's room at about 1:15pm. A nurse was attending to her. Linda and I looked at each other, and without another word being said, both of us at the same time said the word "marriage!" (I found out later that Larry had NOT called her.) Like other times through the years, it was a magical moment—like brain waves emanating from Larry miles away had hit Linda and me. Then I said to Linda, whose eyes were opened very wide: "Should we get married?" and she said emphatically, "Yes!"

I immediately sat down and got out my cellphone, and dialed Google. I searched for a Justice of the Peace who could do marriages. The first number to come up was an 818 area code. I dialed it:

"Hello."

"Hi. Can you do marriages?"

"Yes. Why?"

"Because I want to get married."

"OK. When?"

"This afternoon."

"This afternoon? Where are you?"

I told him.

"OK. Can you give me an hour or so? I'm in the middle of something. But I have all the documents, and stamps, and my license; you will see everything."

"OK. Let me give you directions to parking and where to go in the hospital to my wife's room."

Which I did. He affirmed he would be there. Next, I called my good buddy Jean C., a well-educated Frenchman who has been living in LA for forty years and became a citizen here. He lives less than ten minutes from UCLA Med in Santa Monica.

PART VI

"Jean, it's me Frank. Do you want to be a witness to Linda and me getting married this afternoon?"

"Married? This afternoon? You and Linda? Hell yes! Where are you?"

I told him. He said he would be there in less than one-half hour. Which he was. He showed up with a huge bouquet of flowers, which he put in her lap, as she was in bed. She smiled like the angel she was. Then he showed me his favorite cell phone. He would take pictures of the entire ceremony, which I now have.

"Who is going to marry you?"

"A guy from the from the San Fernando Valley. He's on his way. I think he's a Rabbi."

"Why do you think he's a Rabbi?"

Essentially, dear reader, because I was fortunate enough to grow up in a Jewish neighborhood in Dayton, Ohio. I explained it all to Jean. In 1950, my parents had been looking for a house to buy for the five of us. One long block had all two-storey houses on it, except for one large, beautiful one-story ranch-style house. Dad wanted that house for Mom, because she had a bum knee from an accident playing basketball when she was a teenager. With no stairs to climb inside, this house would be great for Mom. And when Dad found out that it was a Jewish neighborhood, that sealed the deal for him. Dad grew up in Chicago, where there were Jewish kids on his football team. He loved them. Many from the Old Country, all of them tough. Later Dad was an NCO in an Army infantry outfit in WW II and had no sympathy for the persecution of Jewish folks by the Nazis. We were not Jewish, but Dad explained to me: "Frankie, the good Jewish people are very smart, and they place a great emphasis on higher education. I want my kids to grow up in an environment like this." Also, I had been to Israel and Russia in my travels to many lands, and I could hear many accents by non-native English speakers.

"Because, Jean, I could hear an Eastern European and an Israeli accent when he spoke. He told me his name is Josh, as in Joshua. He can do marriages. I will bet that he is a Rabbi, maybe from Russia, and more recently, Israel."

At 4:30pm a large man, almost my height, showed up to Linda's room. He asked for me.

"Hi, Josh, I'm Frank," as I stuck out my hand.

Over the next hour or so, as Josh prepared paperwork and then did the ceremony, there was enough time for small talk and for me to verify that he was from Russia and Israel, and that he was a Rabbi. That all made me happy because as a kid, growing up near three Jewish Temples within walking distance of our house, I got to know several Rabbi's. I always thought, if I ever get married, I want to get married by a Rabbi! Of course, if you have read the earlier stories about us, dear reader, you already know that this will be our second marriage.

So Linda and I filled out all of the papers for Josh, he verified that all was correct, while Jean was busy taking pictures of all of it, and finally Josh said, in his heavy accent:

"OK. I have all the paperwork, everything has been stamped and has my Notary seal, and that all took about twenty-five minutes or so, longer than the marriage ceremony will take. So Frank, you go over by Linda."

I went over and stood by Linda in her bed and held her hand. We looked at each other smiling, our love for each other thick in the air, visible in the room. Josh did the reading of the first part of the ceremony, and then he read what he called the "rules of marriage" and the vows: "Frank, do you take this lady Linda to be your lawful wedded wife . . . " and the same for Linda about me. A few more words. Then he said "Now you are married. Frank, you may kiss your bride!"

By now we were both laughing and crying like babies, and holding each other, and smiling and kissing and saying "I love you" to each other. And Jean has photos of all of these wonderful moments, the happiest moments of both of our lives. We were so happy just to have known each other for so long and having been together for so long. It was joyous and sublime!

And when I drive alone up Third Street between Rose Avenue and Ocean Park Boulevard in The Ocean Park area of Santa Monica, next to Venice, and see the mature Bottle Brush trees growing in the grassy parkway beside the sidewalks, I think of Linda. We had only known each other about a year when together we got the City of Santa Monica to plant those trees on the street, over fifty years ago. I have explained this event in an earlier story in this book. Sweet memory.

Back in Linda's room—AKA: the Wedding Chapel—we all said thanks and goodbye to Josh for what he had done for Linda and me. Linda and I looked at each other and cried a little and laughed a little and just enjoyed being together. This was on Tuesday afternoon, September 6th. As the evening wore on, nurses brought her liquids to drink, and chipped ice, which she liked to dissolve in her mouth when it was dry and she was thirsty. She continued to work sitting up in the bed, her laptop computer in her lap. Sometimes she wrote short letters, or answered her emails, but more often she was working on a poem or editing poems she had already written. She was also thinking about presentations into September, October, November. She was amazing—she was not giving up! Later in the evening, sometime between 8:00pm and 9:00pm, a nurse came by and gave her an IV sedative. It would ease her nascent pain and help her sleep. It had been a big, wonderful day for both of us! I reluctantly went home to get some sleep.

Wednesday went into Thursday went into Friday. She was working on her computer after 9:00am for a while, a couple of hours, then would need some sleep. Not eating, just drinking, or sucking juice. Some friends would visit during the week for a short time, or text her, or email her, or call. One dear old friend who lived with us on Wavecrest Avenue in Venice as early as 1970 when we were all students, Joseph was his name, spent two days visiting. He was very kind and patient, so when she needed a nap, he would take a break, hang around, and come see her again a little while later. Sometime after she had passed away, he told me that those two days visiting with Linda were probably the most meaningful days in his entire life. She knew what was happening to her, she was at peace with it, not afraid, and expressed more concern for me than for herself. As Joseph described the conversations to me, a sublime feeling came over me that I had seldom had before, as I realized how profoundly loving she was about how her life had turned out to be, and that I had been part of it. Despite the abuse and neglect, she had experienced in her early youth, and never believing that anyone would love her or value her, she was thankful that she had been wrong about that, both in her public and private lives. Other friends came to visit her as well, including dear Patty, who had known us for forty-three years, with the aim to bring some joy into Linda's room, which she did.

On Saturday things took a nasty turn, a portent. Her legs were swelling and hurting. She asked me to rub them from her ankles to her hips with a certain cream, to alleviate the pain, which I did. I also had to give her, little by little, small pieces of ice in her mouth, to ease her dryness. She was being given morphine IV to sleep, and again in the middle of the night. But during the day she was still working on her poetry on her computer.

On Sunday I was in her room during the day, trying to help her, and decided to stay there all night. I tried to sleep in a chair, which was miserable. By Monday morning I was a wreck. I helped her a bit, gave her some ice bits, and went home to take a shower and get something to eat. I made a few phone calls, then went back to the hospital. I rubbed her legs some more and gave her ice. At one point she seemed settled down a bit, as they had given her a little medicine for pain. On Monday afternoon I left the hospital to run a couple of errands and came back later in the afternoon. I stayed with her for a while after they gave her morphine IV for pain and to sleep. I massaged her legs again with the cream; her legs were more swollen now. They would give her another injection of morphine in the middle of the night, as they had been doing. By now I was so exhausted I could hardly see, and I was afraid to drive home to get a little sleep, but I did. I fell asleep in my clothes, intending to return to the hospital in the early am Tuesday.

At 4:45am Tuesday morning, September 13th, 2022, my cell phone rang: "Hello."

"Hello, Mr. Lutz. This is UCLA Hospital Santa Monica calling. I am so sorry to tell you that your dear wife Linda has passed away at 4:40am this morning. I am sorry."

"Yes. Thank you. So am I. I will be there."

I was in a daze. Not much sleep, not eating anything for two days except liquids. Worry and anxiety, the pain of Linda, the pain of me. The woman who had been everything to me since 1968, was now gone. Must go see her, she needs me now as before. I guess I was in denial, too hopeful, that she would go on, could go on, survive longer, maybe even rally. I had made it a point during the eleven days she had been there to visit all three nursing shifts. I talked to the staff, showed them pictures of Linda and articles about Linda, told them she was very special, loved by a lot of people, and she would be an easy patient for them to take care of. And she was. The staff was very kind and caring to her.

When I got back to her room, she was laying peacefully in the bed, wrapped to the waist in a white shroud, dressed in a sleeping gown, arms folded across her stomach, her long and beautiful and talented hands one on top of the other. I took one hand and kissed it. I looked at her beautiful and now very thin face for a while. She was still beautiful. She was at peace, no more pain, no more wondering how long she would be alive. This was the woman for whom I had changed the trajectory of my life back in 1968. I had been lucky to have had that intuition. For as my buddy Tony from Chicago had told me twenty years before: "Frank, Linda was your father's gift to you from his grave."

So I said to this beautiful poet as she lay there: "Linda, I will always love you, I will love you forever. And as Dante followed Virgil when Virgil beckoned him, when you see my time is near, beckon me like Virgil beckoned Dante, and I will follow you. And I will find you again, my love."

Then I placed her hand back on her other hand, stood up and bent over and kissed her on her forehead. And said: "Goodbye, my Linda."

I turned and walked to the door, stopped, and turned around to look at her one more time. Then I left. That was the last time I would ever see my Linda . . . until . . .

Back in this life:

A few days later I looked in her laptop computer to see when she had made her last entries. Her last entry was a poem she was working on at 2:20pm on Monday afternoon, September 12th. She died at 4:40am on Tuesday, September 13th, fourteen hours and twenty minutes later. She never wanted to stop, she wanted always to be a poet, she wanted to be heard. And those who heard her thought she was magnificent.

Frank A. Lutz
co-author. editor. husband.

EPILOGUE

Over the years—decades—people have asked me about Linda, her background, where she is from, how we met, and so forth.

Linda J. Albertano had her first poem published in the early 1960s in Orange County, California when she was nineteen years old. During the following sixty-one years, she would develop prominence in poetry, performance art, music and film. She performed and worked her arts in the USA and other parts of the Western Hemisphere, Europe and Africa. The number of venues, theaters, and stadiums where she performed, plus small clubs and private showings, can be counted in the hundreds. Her poems were published in dozens of magazines and poetry anthologies.

Linda spent the first eight years of her life with her family in Utah, Montana, and finally Denver. At age eight, when her brother Jim was only four years old, their father abandoned the family and accused their mother Alberta of not being able to care for the children, which was untrue. This is just one reason Linda's support for Women's Rights was unwavering throughout her career in all of her art disciplines.

Alberta was a fine person. Very loving of her children and an artist, as Linda would become. Linda always said, "Any good qualities I have, I got from my mother."

Her father reported Alberta to Denver child "welfare", who took the children and put them into foster homes, and worse, separated them into different homes! Both Linda and her brother Jim would be treated to several years of neglect and abuse in the foster homes, which would have a negative impact on them for the rest of their lives.

Linda was often not allowed to eat meals with the foster family and treated more like a domestic maid than a child. Linda went on to become an Honors student both in high school and in college at University of Colorado, Boulder. At age nineteen her father remarried, and her step-mother refused to fund Linda's University of Colorado tuition or expenses. (Contrary to some misinformation about her, Linda was born on April 17, 1942, and not 1952.)

So her weak-minded father gave her $50.00 in spending money and a one-way ticket to Los Angeles, where Linda knew no one! Linda struggled in LA, doing odd jobs until she was discovered due to her beauty and height, when she started to work doing modeling and some TV work, including as a regular friend of *The Monkees* TV program, as well as *The Ozzie and Harriet* TV show.

For a time, she was also the Space Girl at Disneyland, and she appeared in the movies *Mary Poppins* and *Beach Red*, an Academy Award nominated film. She was also developing her talent as a guitar-playing blues singer. Linda Ronstadt and The Stone Ponies and Taj Mahal recorded at least one of Linda's blues songs called "The Two-ten Train" on one of their albums. During the mid-1960s Linda made two trips with the USO during the Vietnam War as a dancer-singer with an all-girls troupe to Vietnam, Cambodia, Thailand, South Korea, and Japan.

In 1966 she enrolled at UCLA to complete her higher education and get a degree. Because of her excellent grades, obvious intelligence, and lack of family support, UCLA gave Linda a grant and scholarship money to attend that great university. Her Senior Class film was voted by students and faculty in the Film Department the Best Film of the Year when she graduated in 1971.

When I met Linda she had no family support, nor help from anyone else. She did all of this on her own.

It is also interesting to note that Linda Albertano was the first female member of Gold's Gym, Venice, having joined in 1970 when she was in UCLA film school, to get her arms stronger for carrying heavy camera equipment.

POSTSCRIPT

A fact that I did not include in this story about Linda is that I had been writing poetry for several years before we met in 1968. I started writing poetry in the early 1960s during my time sailing with the Woods Hole Oceanographic Institution in Massachusetts as a student scientist. I sailed on the RV Atlantis and then on the RV Atlantis II, around the globe. I also was writing poetry during my time in 1964 at the University of Perugia in Italy, as well as when I was in school in France and Germany. Linda had read my poetry many times and loved it. I wrote about war, flying (I have a commercial pilot's license), history, and mystical events that have come to me in my dreams. But with Linda I never pushed to perform my poetry, because I did not want her to think that I was competing with her, or encroaching on her intellectual territory, so close to home. So I stayed in the background and supported her and her efforts. She deserved my support in all parts of her life. So the fact of our meeting on that cold, dark, rainy February night in 1968 when she stopped to pick me up from hitch-hiking looms even larger in our fates.

The conversation with my dad about the importance of poetry (his own Master's Thesis was on the US Civil War and the great American poet Robert Frost); the thousands of cars going by me on the streets that night when she stopped for me; her decision to wait for me and to honk again, more aggressively; the fact that she was a poet. How many other cars that night could have had such a rare person as a poet in them? And the fact that I was, still am, a poet. My buddy Tony Gutilla had it right: Linda was my dad's gift to me from his grave. But she considered me to be a gift to her, too, from someone, maybe some ancestor, who cared for her.

So the proof is "in the pudding" so they say: 55 years together, through good times and hard times. I have been told many times that our relationship was "meant to be". Yes, I agree.

What do you think Reader? ... email me at **FrankALutz@gmail.com**

—*FL*

AN IDEA FOR THOSE WHO GRIEVE

The main thrust of this document is to help those who have lost a loved one to understand that they are not alone, and that—believe it or not—human and scientific systems are being used today for the living to possibly get into contact with your dearly departed. Furthermore, with training and practice it may be possible for you to learn this skill.

It happened to me: I lost my dear wife Linda, and I learned how to have direct contact with her. I write this document to help you, dear reader, and to honor my Linda.

After Linda passed away on September 13th, 2022, I was in shock, severe grief, and depression. I became very busy organizing her various art works and winding down our business. At the same time, I started investigating the process of Afterlife communications. But in late November I received a call from a dear lady friend of ours who lives in Denver, with a surprising story she had to tell me. She told me that for many years on occasion she would hear a voice in her head, usually telling her that some member of her large family was in distress or had a serious health problem.

This particular night she had been asleep, and at 2:00am she was awakened by a loud voice in her head, yelling out her name and my name, and the voice woke her up. The voice was Linda, telling our friend that she had been trying to get a message to me, but my grief was so intense that she could not get through to me. I had read that severe grief could be an impediment to receiving Afterlife communications. So Linda wanted our friend to convey some information to me, which our friend was happy to do. In fact, our friend had written down two pages of notes, based on what Linda had said to tell me.

Our friend faxed me the notes. Linda wanted me to know that she was OK, that she was being well looked after, that the place where she was living was quite beautiful, full of peace and kindness, and that yes, the people there looked human, but had no bodies; they were indeed Spirits, but could look completely human, with clothing on, and so forth. And their "minds" (i.e.: consciousness) worked quite well, they could think, write, create, etc. Obviously, Linda's contact with our friend and the notes to me were surprising, but I had already started to read about the Afterlife, so the communication made sense, according to what I had been reading.

In addition to my busy days, I started reading voraciously late at night, as I am a fast reader and have a good retention rate. My readings by various authors who were involved in various aspects of the Afterlife science were to give me a sound understanding of what was real, and how it had been proven. In addition to my reading, over the next few months I took various online courses in Afterlife communication techniques, and two courses in meditation, including one in Transcendental Meditation, which I highly recommend.

By early November I had heard about and investigated the process of communication with departed loved ones, otherwise known as Afterlife Communications (ALC). I thought to myself that as desperate as I was to communicate with Linda, she must be equally desperate to communicate with me, after all these years of loving each other. So I decided to start researching what I would come to understand was an intense, widely and deeply studied and researched science.

So I started reading about the science of quantum mechanics and its discoveries since the beginning of the 19th century as to how the world works on a subatomic level, a key to the development of understanding ALC. I went on to read books by psychologists and parapsychologists, medical professionals, researchers, practicing Mediums, people who had near death experiences (NDE's), and people who had actually communicated with their departed loved ones (DLOs). Between November 2022 and the end of September 2023 I would read forty-three books. In addition, in January 2023, I started taking online classes in the science of ALC, instructed by professors, researchers, and mediums with advanced academic credentials and degrees, and who are some prominent names in the science: R. Craig Hogan, Gary Schwartz, Suzanne Gieseman, Kriss Kevorkian, Elizabeth Raver, Hillary Michaelson, et al. I continue to read and study the science of ALC. To date, 3/20/2024, I have read fifty-seven books on this science of communication.

Now, on to the main purpose of this document: I believe that most people in the world at some point in their lives lose a dearly beloved person, a relative or a friend, and the loss is devastating to them. I further believe that many people would like to maintain contact with the person who they lost, but don't know how to do that, and/or don't believe it can be done. I would like to show or explain to those folks that it can be done, that there exists plenty of evidence to that effect, and that I can explain to them the science and how it works to allow them to make contact. I would start briefly with an explanation of the science that helps to make communication possible, and then describe the process of communication, and finally, what a person must do to be able to partake in the communication.

I also work with several Mediums in order to begin contacting Linda; I have stuck with the two best Mediums, both of whom are ladies who are well-educated, and have been doing medium ship work for decades, and are the best at it. I continue reading and taking courses in this science of Afterlife communications.

IN THE BEGINNING:
Early in the 19th century, a German physicist named Max Planck discovered what came to be known as subatomic particles. A couple of decades later a Danish physicist named Niels Bohr expanded on Planck's work. Thus, the theory of quantum mechanics had its beginnings. Both of those scientists would later be honored with a Nobel Prize. All things in the universe are made of molecules which are made of atoms and subatomic particles, smaller than atoms. We cannot see atoms; we must observe them with very sophisticated equipment and spectroscopes. As to subatomic particles that also reside inside the molecular field along with the atoms, they cannot be seen either; in fact, only their action or what they do can be seen, as they can be millions of times smaller than their atoms. This may be hard for you to imagine, but these tiny items that make up the matter in the world—including you and me, animals, rocks, plants, and so forth—have enormous energy, essentially electro-magnetic energy and light. This is all about matter and energy in the world at the most fundamental level. It is claimed by science and physicists that the power of subatomic particles and their electromagnetic energy collectively can be more powerful than atomic energy. And that is all we are, in our most basic form: electromagnetic energy and light.

Why is this important? Because that is what messages, communication is—electromagnetic energy and light. When we speak in person, when we talk on the telephone, when we talk telepathically, it is all electromagnetic energy and light. Light travels at over 186,000 miles PER SECOND. So when a 17-year-old boy on vacation from his home in Germany comes to visit Venice, California 7,000 miles away and gets bitten on his leg by a shark while swimming in the Pacific Ocean and thinks of his mother, she at home in Berlin can feel a message of pain in her leg and sense that it is from her son, instantly. The message was sent telepathically, or via mental telepathy, which is moved at the speed of light because of electromagnetic energy's power; the atmosphere of the universe is full of powerful electromagnetic subatomic energy, fulfilling many purposes. Intentional telepathic messages from one person to another are the way in which a living human being here on Earth is able to speak with his/her DLO, who is also living, but in an altered or "transformed" form, in the Afterlife, as pure consciousness in a human form. Furthermore, the scientists and professionals who work with Afterlife concepts do not say that when we pass to the next life that we have "died". They say that we have simply "transformed" or "transitioned" into a different type or form of existence, and that we are very much alive and accessible for communication. They also say that we can take on other forms, but essentially our thought processes, our memory, and other abilities are all intact. Why would that be? Because we still have our consciousness, and our thought processes, reasoning, communication skills, and so forth.

The scientists also do not refer to the Afterlife as Heaven or Hell. They refer to the beings there as Spirits; they use religion-neutral language, as just like here on our Earth there are many different types of people and their religions in the Afterlife.

Where do we get all of this information about the Afterlife? Basically, from two sources: from what we call NDEs, or people who have had a Near Death Experience (NDE); and from our DLOs in communications with their loved ones here, as they describe life in the Afterlife. Let's start with the NDE.

Someone in your family may have had an NDE. Let's say it's Uncle Joe, who goes into hospital for a heart operation. During the procedure, poor Uncle Joe dies. As the medical team is frantically trying to revive him, Uncle Joe feels himself leaving his body, and floating up toward the ceiling of the operating room. From the ceiling he can look down on the medical team as they work on him. After a couple of minutes Uncle Joe decides to go back down to the area around his body and try to talk to somebody, but nobody can hear him, so he tries to touch one of them. But his hand goes through the body of the medical person, unnoticed. So then he tries to move the gurney where his body is lying. But again, his hand goes through the gurney. So Uncle Joe realizes something is different, very different. Next, he feels himself floating up toward the ceiling again, and moving on to somewhere else. After a short time, he sees the entrance to a tunnel ahead of him, and he enters it, not under his own power, but rather he is lifted into the tunnel. The tunnel is dark inside, and Uncle Joe feels himself floating forward for a while, he does not know for how long. After some time, he sees a light at the end of the tunnel. He continues to float toward it, until he comes to an end, where people help him out of the tunnel. As he emerges from the tunnel, he sees a group of friendly looking and acting people who are helping him, including some of his recognizable deceased relatives. The physical environment is described later by Uncle Joe as quite beautiful, much like the Earth and at the same time different. He is there for a while, being treated well and made comfortable. Afterwards, an official looking person approaches him speaking kindly to him. The person gently explains to him: "Uncle Joe, it's not your time yet. Your work on Earth is not finished yet. We need to send you back."

With that, he is put back in the tunnel, and sometime later—the NDEs never know how long these episodes last—he finds himself back in the operating room, lying face up on the gurney, with his eyes just opening, and all of the medical staff looking down at him, happy that he has survived. None of them know about or even suspect the trip that he has just been on.

The research shows that approximately 98% of the surveyed NDEs describe the same sort of experience, worldwide. The NDE experience can vary widely in terms of time the person has this experience; it might last for only a few minutes, or much longer. The longest time a person was "dead" has been witnessed and recorded as seven days, and it happened to an American doctor, a brain surgeon named Dr. Eben Alexander. It happened several years ago, and since then he has written and spoken about his experience. At last report, Dr. Alexander is alive and well and practicing medicine on the East Coast of the USA. What is more remarkable about people like Dr. Alexander and others who have experienced NDE is that even though they were dead for a while, they actually remembered their death experience, and can recount it to professional medical people; when you die, your memory bank stops working. So while you are alive, some of your memory is obviously stored outside your brain, as well as partially inside it. After you are "on the other side" your internal memory bank no longer works.

There are several well researched books about the NDE experiences of many people. I can recommend some of the books about NDEs that I have read.

Now let's move on to what we hear from our DLOs about life in the Afterlife. My own experience in communicating with my dear wife Linda is consistent with the reports I have read about communications between other people on Earth and their DLOs.

So how do I recommend that you start to learn how to communicate with your DLO? To start, I recommend that you learn how to meditate, or take a course in meditation. I recommend Transcendental Meditation. Why TM? Because in my experience it was the meditation style that helped me get my mind the clearest and empty of trash and clutter, as well as allowing me to get deeper into the quiet parts of my mind. I also suggest that you start to read about this science. Of the fifty-seven books on the subject that I have read, I can recommend probably fifteen to twenty that were most helpful; but if you are uncomfortable with science, I would not recommend the two books on quantum mechanics and subatomic theory.

During this early phase of your involvement, I also suggest that you start to identify who it is in the Afterlife that you want to contact, and why. I would also recommend that you seek out at least two Mediums who you have researched and feel good about, as being persons who might help you contact your DLO. You can research them online, and they do not need to live near you, nor do you need to have an in-person session with them. In fact, the less they know about you, the better. Of my two ladies, one lives in California, the other lives in Connecticut, and I have never met either of them in person. We do all of our work by phone. When you contact them give them the least information about yourself as possible, like, your name and very little more.

More than likely, you will then be invited for a Reading, or a situation where you are on one phone talking to the Medium who is on his/her phone, and who will be in a trance-like state that will be an asset to the communication. The Medium will then take a bit of time to try to make contact with your DLO, having very little information about your DLO. The Medium will be relying on his/her various trained "senses" or a set of trained feelings and intuitive help, in order to make contact with your DLO. This is when the fun starts, because sometimes anything can happen! Members of your family from generations past may show up; your past and passed away pet dog might show up; Uncle Joe might show up. When all this time you wanted only to speak with your old Granny who took care of you when you were a kid. But eventually your Medium will make contact with Granny, and the dialogue between you, the Medium and Granny will begin. During the session other people may show up just to say Hello. The sessions typically last for about an hour. Then it will be over, and more than likely you will be very glad you did it. And you will be amazed by the whole process.

I believe your next step is to ask your Medium, or research it yourself, about a school or instruction as to how you can learn to contact your DLO by yourself. Then you will have as resources for connection to both your Medium and you, like I have found to be both beneficial and personally very wonderful.

RECOMMENDED BOOKS TO READ
most of which can be bought on Kindle, for a lower price:

Your Eternal Self by R. Craig Hogan
Proof of Heaven by Dr. Eben Alexander
Afterlife Communication edited by R. Craig Hogan, an Anthology
The Crossover Experience by D J Kadagian
The Intention Experiment by Lynne McTaggart
Become an Empath with These 8 Brain Training Tips by Steve Phillips-Waller

ONE FINAL NOTE TO YOU, DEAR READER:
As I tell people, before my dear Linda passed on, I did not know much at all about Afterlife communications. But after she passed, that topic kept getting my attention. So I surmised, if this is for real, and Linda has found out about it, she must be as desperate to communicate with me as I am to communicate with her. So in early November, 2022 I started reading—a lot—about it. By the end of December, I had read fourteen books on the subject in nine weeks. In January 2023, I started taking online classes and Zoom classes on the subject, while continuing to read, plus doing various tasks to archive Linda's art and to create a scholarship for poets under her name.

As I have mentioned, I wanted to understand the science behind this communication science, so I started reading about quantum mechanics theory, subatomic particles, and so forth. It was very useful to me, but is not necessary for you to read, to benefit from this wonderful communication system. I also read books by scientific researchers, psychologists and parapsychologists, medical doctors, Mediums, and by people who have had NDE experiences and/or have communicated directly with their DLOs (Departed Loved Ones). I also had Medium contact with Linda, with the help of several Mediums, and decided early on to stick with two lady Mediums, one in California and one in Connecticut, both of whom are outstanding. I work with them over the phone to do Readings (i.e.: conversations) with Linda.

Needless to say, I have benefitted greatly emotionally and psychologically from my communications with Linda, both via Medium and directly one-on-one. She seems happy in the Afterlife, as she describes it to me. She has explained to me how she lives there, what it looks like, and what she does, and about friends she has made there, and members of both of our families she spends time with there. I can highly recommend that you look into it, if you lose someone you love, and want to maintain contact with them.

ABOUT FRANK LUTZ

Frank is co-author of the book *On the Life of Linda J. Albertano: From Trauma to High Art*. In January 1968, he is in Hollywood, and Frank's life changes forever—he meets Linda Albertano! Linda and Frank got married for the second time when she was in UCLA Hospital on September 6th, 2022. It was the very happiest moment of both of their lives! She introduced him to UCLA, where she had been studying film and performance art.

Linda and Frank were married twice and the second time, after 55 years together, was when she was in UCLA Hospital on September 6th, 2022. It was the happiest moment of both of their lives! Sadly, Linda passed away on September 13, 2022. She introduced Frank to UCLA, where she was studying film and performance art. Frank graduated Summa Cum Laude, was elected to Phi Beta Kappa, and received a Graduate Fellowship in Philosophy. He became a Council member at the UCLA Center for Medieval and Renaissance Studies and remains so today. Since 2002, he has been a Distinguished Scholar at the Vatican for his research into an event occurring in 1279 AD. He possesses a Vatican passport and is called Dottore Lutz in the Vatican Secret Archives. Frank also has a commercial pilot's license, and FAA pilot instructor certificates. Currently, he's diving into the science of quantum mechanics and exploring ALC (After Life Communications) with Linda. He is a poet, narrative writer, and successful business owner in Venice, California.

PART VII
THE LINDA J. ALBERTANO FELLOWSHIP FOR WOMEN POETS

PERSONAL NOTES

IT ALL BEGAN WITH CHERRY SOUP

PART VII

INTRODUCING:
THE LINDA J. ALBERTANO FELLOWSHIP FOR WOMEN POETS

An annual event to be held at Beyond Baroque, the world famous poetry venue in Venice, California.

After Linda passed away on September 13th, 2022, her husband Frank Lutz created the Linda J. Albertano Fellowship for Women Poets at Beyond Baroque, with the help of their Director, Mr. Quentin Ring. Each year around the anniversary of Linda's birthdate, which is April 17th, a monetary prize will be awarded to the winner poet who submits her poetry to Beyond Baroque's panel of judges. This year, 2024, the first winner, Ms. Abbi Page, was announced and awarded her prize at a ceremony on April 13th in Beyond Baroque's main building. In addition to celebrating Linda's birthday and awarding the prize for poetry, Frank Lutz introduced the first book of Linda's poetry, called *On the Life of Linda J. Albertano: From Trauma to High Art*. Above and left are a few photos scenes from the event during the evening of the prize award.

AND FINALLY, ON A PERSONAL NOTE FROM THE AUTHOR, FRANK LUTZ:

The two lovely people above, Kat Georges and her husband, Peter Calaftes hail from New York City, and during the past several decades have been leaders in the American DADA art movement. They publish a book annually, a compendium of DADA and other poetry, called Maintenant, a French word for "now". They were dear pals of Linda's, with whom they had a mutual admiration society. Kat is also a book designer who helped my wonderful team and me, put this book and the first one, *On the Life of Linda J. Albertano* together, along with my wonderful team of Ms. Deborah Granger of Quiet Time Publishing, publisher and producer, and Mr. Alex Carmona, technical/computer wiz. Although Kat and Peter may look gleeful and slightly deranged in the photo, I can assure you they are harmless and charming.

PART VII

BOOKS BY LINDA J. ALBERTANO AND FRANK LUTZ

Quiet Time Publishing is pleased to publish the Linda J. Albertano collection, a trio of tributes to the poet and performance artist, along with work by her husband of 55 years, Frank Lutz.

ON THE LIFE OF LINDA J. ALBERTANO FROM TRAUMA TO HIGH ART
**By Linda J. Albertano with Frank Lutz;
Foreword by Suzanne Lummis**

On the Life of Linda J. Albertano features photos, memorabilia, images, and performance reviews from Linda's personal journal. But most important is the collection of stories, poems, and provocative prose by both authors.

IT ALL BEGAN WITH CHERRY SOUP
**Poems and Stories by Linda J. Albertano and Frank Lutz;
Foreword by Susan Hayden**

This companion book to *On the Life of Linda J. Albertano*, offers a retrospective of Linda and Frank's written work, including poetry and prose, providing a fascinating look at the creative force that emerged from this one-of-a-kind relationship.

TWO MINDS DESPERATE TO CONNECT: WITH HELP FROM A THIRD ONE
By Elizabeth Raver, Ph.D., Linda J. Albertano, and Frank Lutz

An one-of-a-kind literary work revealing how two lovers, separated by the death of one, have remained in contact, featuring actual transcriptions of "live" conversations between Linda in the Afterlife, Frank on Earth, and Elizabeth, the Medium who helps them. Offers a guide for readers to contact their own departed loved one directly!

For more details, visit
QUIET TIME PUBLISHING
online at **www.quiettimepublishing.com**
or scan the QR code

www.ingramcontent.com/pod-product-compliance
Lightning Source LLC
Chambersburg PA
CBHW051330110526
44590CB00032B/4468